No Problem!

No Problem!

Worldwise Travel Tips for Mature Adventurers

JANICE KENYON

photograhy by E. Ross Henry

ORCA BOOK PUBLISHERS

Canadian Cataloguing in Publication Data
Kenyon, Janice, 1938 –
No problem!

Includes bibliographical references and index.
ISBN 1-55143-080-0

1. Travel. 2. Middle-aged persons — Travel. 3. Aged —Travel. I. Title.
G151.K46 1996 910'2'020846 C95–911190–5

Cover design by Christine Toller
Cover photograph and interior photographs by E. Ross Henry
Edited by Andrew Wooldridge
Printed and bound in Canada

Orca Book Publishers
PO Box 5626, Station B
Victoria, BC V8R 6S4
Canada

Orca Book Publishers
PO Box 468
Custer, WA 98240-0468
USA

10 9 8 7 6 5 4 3 2 1

To everyone who seeks adventure
beyond their armchairs

Table of Contents

Introduction

No Problem!

To travel, take a trip, go on a journey, follow a path ... all indicate traveling from one place to another. An intrepid traveler is resolute, one who moves without fear through an unknown, like Dervla Murphy bicycling in East Africa or Barry Lopez camping on ice floes in the Arctic. Not all travelers are like Murphy or Lopez; many are not even a little intrepid. But for those of us whose curiosity outweighs our fear, to take a trip and leave behind the trappings and complexities of our modern lives is to be free. The gates open and we fly. Where we will stay, what we will see, who we will talk to are unknowns. A large part of the adventure and of the attraction is the uncertainty which quickly becomes joy and wonder at a world opened before us, like a childhood atlas. There is time for assimilation, meditation, appreciation. We reflect, we change. Those insignificant hurdles at home disappear as we gain new understanding of disappearing tropical rain forests or a megalopolis of slums, or stand in awe before giant golden Buddhas that soar to the heavens, like the mountains from which they are carved.

When traveling independently, we are left to our own devices — planning an itinerary and purchasing tickets, arranging financing before and during the trip, gaining knowledge regarding security and health concerns, packing only the clothes and equipment we really need, and ultimately, finding affordable accommodation as well as transportation in countries where the local language is a mystery. Information resources are often difficult to discover, let alone understand. Travel agents can ferret out answers only to specific questions asked by their client; if a client doesn't ask the appropriate question, the information isn't supplied. If an independent traveler doesn't know exactly where or when they are going, a travel agent is of little use. And rarely can seniors glean helpful hints for their specific needs from guidebooks.

No Problem: World-wise travel tips for mature adventurers offers hands-on travel advice for independent, active seniors. Suggestions for when, where, and how are complemented with tips for itinerary planning and security precautions. While preparation for long trips can be daunting, following the checklists of reminders can simplify and assist with those details so necessary if we are to enjoy ourselves once finally away. Health and money are two concerns that vary from country to country, but basic immunization preparation and an understanding of international banking takes the guesswork out of planning and, ultimately, makes one feel more secure. So, let's pack our packs, learn something about international communication systems, and *travel.* Whether for one month or one year, we may find ourselves riding an elephant in Nepal, traveling upriver on a *klotok* in Borneo, or buying handwoven dowry *kilims* from a Turkish carpet merchant after our umpteenth glass of tea. Wherever our wanderings lead, we will most likely find native residents who are eager to share their culture. We will not be sheltered behind barriers of impersonal tour guides and bus drivers, and we will be repeatedly surprised at how many ways there are to say "no problem."

Unless stated otherwise, prices in *No Problem!* are quoted in US dollars, and approximate those listed in 1995. Money markets fluctuate widely, and prices quoted are used merely to give a general indication of basic costs.

"We" in the text refers to myself and Ross Henry, my traveling partner for the past fifteen years. I am the principal note-taker; Ross is the principal photographer. Together we wish you bon voyage!

Chapter One

Comfort

How many stars equal a good night's sleep?

Five-star accommodation is not necessary in order to be comfortable. Avoiding big, expensive hotels means avoiding large groups while also exposing oneself to the indigenous residents of a country — the goal of independent travelers. And for seniors, the big plus is having the time to discover and explore — rushing back to work is not on next Monday's agenda. As you make your way across exotic Southeast Asia or down the Roman roads of Europe, you will find small hotels or guest houses that are family-run, clean, and affordable, ranging from very nice $12 doubles on the Turquoise Coast of Turkey to an $18 double in the Cameron Highlands of Malaysia or a luxurious private *bure* for two in Fiji for $50.

No matter what country, one has to be firm in bargaining for a room rate and also refusing unacceptable dirt or noise conditions. This means "shopping around," and the easiest way to do this is with an agreeable taxi driver. When you arrive, whether disembarking from a train, or bus, or plane, or ferry, touts vying for your patronage can be overwhelming. But there are ways of dealing with unpleasant hawkers and avoiding stressful situations.

The touts' aim is to get your business by hustling you into their vehicle. If you head for the nearest tourist information booth with your bags firmly in tow, you can often avoid the initial push. Even the Kathmandu airport has a tourist booth (which, contrary to what the operator may say, is not entirely independent); at Yogjakarta, Java, Indonesia, the orderly system goes so far as to issue prepaid taxi vouchers once you have selected a place to stay (you can always change your mind when you see your room). The booth operator in Kathmandu will "recommend" a hotel or guesthouse in your price range and attach you to a taxi that, no matter what, is in a falling-apart state but that sooner or later will deliver you to suitable accommodation for just a few dollars' fare. One has to be patient, persevere, and learn how to say NO. Even though the booth operator was sure you did not want the Kathmandu Guest House and that you would gladly accept the $10 not-so-clean, unheated bargain of his choosing, you can persuade the taxi driver to deliver you to the Guest House (which, incidentally, is almost always pre-booked) or an alternative you have chosen after inspection via your now-friendly driver. (During inspection your locked bags remain in the taxi's trunk, and all valuables are attached to your body. See "Security," page 57.)

Taxi drivers in small cities or rural areas *always* know a place to start looking; you may have to settle temporarily for something less than satisfactory if it's late at night or a national holiday. But knowing that a less than agreeable room is short-term can add to the adventure; exploring the next day on foot — and after consulting with fellow travelers — can lead to treasures you didn't know existed. No matter what time of day or night, most taxi drivers will find you something, and in many cases take great pride in assisting you.

Whenever possible, especially in developing countries, use metered taxis. If metered taxis are not available, agree on a price

Temple blessings in Nepal

before starting. If you don't have a clue what a fare should be, ask a fellow traveler who appears to be experienced with the locals, or try to appeal to the honesty of the driver. Being a senior is an advantage; most people truly respect grey hair and wrinkles. The only place I've been ripped off without compunction has been Indonesia, and it would have been avoided if I had persevered to find a metered taxi. Guidebooks comment about taxi systems (whether metered, prepaid, or negotiated) in individual countries. They are worth making note of in case you forget once you arrive, especially if visiting several countries.

Strange as it may seem, many less-developed countries assume a senior backpacker wants the cheapest room available. Perseverance pays off. Sometimes it is difficult to persuade the driver to keep looking, but eventually you'll get that $20 (double) room with a bathtub, plug-in heater or fan plus breakfast instead of the $5 pad with communal shower and cook-you-own breakfast you were shown at the first stop. In New Delhi it took us three tries in the same hotel to arrive at an acceptable room. Finally we agreed on a quiet room with a king-size bed and television for $50. It was over our budget, but we were tired from our Golden Triangle tour (that had come in under budget), and we didn't want to sleep behind the laundry room. All we had to do was convince the management. This happened after reserving at the hotel next door before leaving on the four-day tour and then returning to find a dirty room in the basement being the only available offering. We declined, scouted the neighbourhood, and eventually ensconced ourselves in the $50 room on the tenth floor from where we looked down on anti-government demonstrations in the street the following morning. Perhaps I had a false sense of security, but I was glad I hadn't settled for the ground-floor room behind the laundry. Another plus was the view, of course.

I have heard many seniors complain about poor beds in anything less than five-star hotels. It has been my experience that this is more true in Britain, Ireland, Western Europe and New Zealand than anywhere else in the world. Old saggy mattresses with little or no spring support that long ago saw better nights seem to prevail in the more affordable (and more fun) pensions and bed-and-breakfasts, and I have found two solutions. First, select a room (with twin beds rather than a double) with enough space to slide the mattresses onto the floor. Your back will say many thanks the next day. Second, carry a backpacker's inflatable air mattress or Therm-a-Rest in your bag. It will take up surprisingly little room and provide hours of comfort. I even tote mine in my bicycle panniers when I'm cycling (and I don't carry camping equipment). Exceptions to the "poor bed syndrome" are less-developed countries and most of Asia where comfortable foam or kapok mattresses on firm slabs are the rule. Also, tropical countries that don't imitate Western-style mattresses have cool, firm beds, often complete with mattress pads. Once you find your middle-priced, clean, quiet Shangri-la, you won't want to leave.

Transport on Highway 8, India

When arriving in an expensive, developed city such as Singapore or Hong Kong, it is almost imperative to have a prebooked destination for at least your first night. Prebooked rates are cheaper than arriving unannounced and being subjected to the rack rates (even then, there is room for bargaining *if* a room is available). Keep in mind that the Mercedes air-conditioned taxis from the Singapore airport are expensive (this is not the place to "shop around" via taxi), and also that busy cities such as Singapore, New Delhi, Cairo, and Rome are always overbooked and accommodation even in five-star hotels is difficult to obtain upon arrival any time of the year.

Developed destinations such as Paris, New York City, and London boast inexpensive self-catering flats or studio apartments for rent for a prolonged period of stay (usually for at least one week), and these are not difficult to arrange. Organizations that rent apartments to travelers advertise in leading newspapers and periodicals; consult the Toronto *Globe and Mail*, *New York Times* (classified, travel, and book review sections), *Manchester Guardian*, and travel magazines. Guidebooks sometimes contain this kind of information; browse through the indexes, bibliographies, and appendixes in your favorite travel bookstore and local library.

Computer buffs with modems can tap into several data bases

that carry travel information, including accommodation available around the world. America On-line, Fido Net, CompuServe, and Seniors Network are some examples available. A word of caution: Never reveal credit card numbers to any computer system.

There are numerous US and British, plus a few Canadian, travel businesses that specialize in renting villas on the Costa Del Sol, farm houses in Tuscany, cottages in the Cotswolds, mini-chateaux in Provence, even seaside apartments in Turkey. When it comes to exorbitant hotel rates in Europe, a week shared between two couples on a Tuscan farm during the shoulder season can be a very comfortable bargain (in more ways than one). Travel magazines and newsletters carry listings (see "Appendix A").

House exchanges are another option. Companies that specialize in home exchanges establish their own rules and regulations. Investigate the reliability of the company (references, business association memberships) and fully understand the company's requirements before committing your home (see "Appendix C" for addresses to contact for more information).

Getting around when not attached to a tour coach

Just because you're able to support your own pack on your back doesn't mean you have to carry it around the world. Walking from the train to a taxi with a heavy bag is far enough, and "shopping around" for accommodation via taxi in less-developed countries doesn't cost much. In large, more developed cities, small hotels and guest houses are generally clustered in a particular area to which you can be delivered by taxi and then proceed on foot. In the seventh arrondissement of Paris there are at least a dozen hostelries within two city blocks from which to choose. See the previous section for more tips on finding accommodation via taxis.

Local taxis also offer local history lessons, often laced with local gossip. Taxi drivers can be a wealth of information, although their knowledge may be jaded by personal political views that the listener needs to acknowledge with agreeable smiles. Never an-

Catching a ferry, Fiji style

tagonize a taxi driver! My taxi stories include running out of gas in pitch black 5 A.M. darkness on the back roads of Bali; having a flat tire and no working tire jack on a pot-holed country road in Fiji; grinding to a halt with an engine breakdown in the US Virgin Islands; being stopped by police because of a beginning flat tire (it progressed to the real thing) in Nairobi — all on the way to an airport or ferry dock. And I've never missed a plane or boat because of taxi mishaps. Getting upset with the driver when breakdowns happen makes things worse. Try to arrive at a solution that meets your needs, as in getting to the airport on time. In Fiji we hailed a passing car that delivered us to the beach-cum-ferry landing while the driver cheerfully looked for rocks to prop his car and change the tire; in the Virgin Islands, we simply flagged down another taxi (they were plentiful there) while our driver busied himself under the hood, and in Nairobi we waited in the shade of a roadside stall for the few minutes it took to change the tire. Bali was tricky, but the driver, our mini tour guide of the day before, was committed to getting us to the airport on time so he approached the one house with a light burning, retrieved a can of gas, and we arrived with time to spare. Allowing enough time is essential; strange destinations in the wee hours of the morning or in crowded cities require extra time — sometimes hours. You may not like hanging around airports, but those extra free moments are worth a lot of stress. A rule when traveling on your own: always have a good book in your carry-on.

There is no doubt that traveling by local bus is cheaper than taxi fares, but buses aren't always practical (especially when catching a 6 A.M. flight or transporting your bags short distances). Investigate local transportation systems before you go, and budget accordingly, plus a little extra. You may find yourself in a small-town bus stop in Malaysia waiting for a bus that won't run for another two days, and there's no place to stay. Somehow, when buses disappear, taxis miraculously appear, and you can usually negotiate an acceptable fare to your destination. Sit back and enjoy the ride.

Hiring a car and driver for what seem like long distances is normal practice in countries like Nepal and India where public transportation is next to impossible to use. It's true that Nepalese public buses operate almost on schedule; they will even deliver you to one side of a landslide that is blocking the highway and have another bus waiting on the other side — after you have traipsed across the obstructing debris carrying your own bags. But hired cars are almost as cheap as the buses, infinitely more comfortable, and the driver will assist you over the road block. In India hired cars for mini tours (three to five days) are the norm and very inexpensive. They can be arranged in a regulated manner (as regulated as is possible in India) at the government tourist information booths at major airports, and they are the best option for seniors traveling in India. Ask for air conditioning and be sure it works. Being able to keep the windows closed has advantages even if the temperature isn't 90°F (32°C) — sticky fingers will not invade your space, and there is a barrier between you and the dust and sometimes-crushing traffic.

Buses in Thailand boast videos and continuous music — all at top volume! Deafening American rock tapes and/or kung fu videos require ear plugs or your own Walkman. Carrying a few ounces of a personal sound system is a big bonus here. There is great comfort in a little Mozart while leaving smoggy Bangkok

Maasai women selling beadwork, Tanzania

behind, and you can always catch the video shoot-outs and punch-ups out of the corner of your eye if you need diversion during an eight-hour journey. Thai buses are air-conditioned and fairly comfortable. They are run by competing private companies, so try to pick one with reclining seats that work and air conditioning that looks as if it won't break down. These buses stop for meal breaks at designated restaurants that are not necessarily clean, and the food not always edible. Before leaving, pack some snack food from the stall selling packaged goodies that you discovered near your hotel.

When traveling in Africa, research local transportation carefully. We knew we had to travel by bus from Nairobi, Kenya to Arusha, Tanzania to connect with our pre-arranged safari, but we only accidentally learned from an ex-resident of Kenya that it's best to take a private rather than public bus. This was easily arranged through our hotel in Nairobi. We went through the Kenya/Tanzania border quickly and efficiently, and for just a few dollars more than the local bus, were much more comfortable. Alas, on the return trip, our private minibus broke down and we were rescued on the Maasai Steppe (while we were pushing our stalled vehicle backwards up a hill) by a stuffed-to-overflowing local bus. We were glad to get to Nairobi four hours later, but the driver's assistant had insisted that we take seats away from the local passengers as soon as he could arrange it. We were white tourists, grey-haired and wrinkled, and there was no arguing. On arrival at the city bus station, the driver cautioned us to guard our packs and get directly into a taxi to our hotel. I had a guardian angel, even if I had been shoved into someone else's seat unwillingly.

The bus system in Turkey is probably one of the cheapest and most efficient in the world, but don't believe it when they say "air conditioned." Invariably, the air conditioning is turned off when climbing a hill, and Turkey is full of mountains, so be prepared. And summertime is hot! Take advantage of being a senior and travel shoulder season; May and October are perfect months for this most interesting and most affordable crossroads of the world.

Many guidebooks offer transportation information and advice for individual countries. Study these carefully and try to discern how to travel efficiently and comfortably. Often it's by plane: Garuda Indonesia offers a Visit Indonesia Decade Pass (1993 to 2003) to bona fide residents of a foreign country; Fiji Air offers inter-island passes that can be purchased on arrival in Nadi. These arrangements require research before booking. Obviously, you will plan ahead in a country as large as Indonesia, but you also need to have an idea before you leave home of which islands you want to visit in Fiji as the flight times are fixed (but incredibly cheap). See "Planning: Through the skies, over land, or across the water" (page 49), for more hints on air passes.

South Pacific destinations such as Tonga, Fiji, and the Cook Islands have inter-island flights on small planes that board according to careful weight restrictions. Be at the airport one and one half to two hours early! Two hundred kilo Tongans plus their baggage leave little room for much else, and you *will be* bumped if the weight capacity is filled.

Train travel is often unique, usually fun, and in most European countries, reliable. Eurail and Britrail passes offer considerable senior discounts. Prices of train fares, including Eurail passes, have increased dramatically over the past few years, and it's worth doing homework regarding renting or leasing a car versus traveling by train. Time is often the deciding factor; long-term (four weeks or more) car rentals are relatively inexpensive from particular countries (for instance, Germany is usually cheaper than Austria). But if you have only two weeks for Amsterdam and Paris, the train will be your best bet. For that special once-in-a-lifetime thrill, hop the Orient Express to Venice.

Because train travel in less-developed countries is subject to unstable politics as well as funding, established routes — even very popular ones — that have been disrupted by flooding or other natural disasters may not run again until there has been a change of government. Don't rely on guidebooks for up-to-date information. Find a travel agent that specializes in the particular place you want to travel by train, and ask specifically how recent their information is and where it has come from. If it's the same guidebook you got from the library, keep searching; the most recent guidebook's input is at least six months old. Over-burdened systems in heavily populated countries such as India and Indonesia speak for themselves — buying a first-class ticket for a private sleeper compartment is no guarantee that several fellow travelers will not be firmly settled on your bunk before you arrive. This is the place to fly or hire a car and driver. If you're considering something like Russia's Trans-Siberian Special, talk to someone who has done it before you complete your final plans. Russia's interpretation of first-class luxury and your interpretation are probably worlds apart, literally. This may be a situation which can be tolerated for a shorter distance than all the way across the steppes of Siberia.

Planning a mature traveler's budget

How much money do I need? How do I get it? What are the hidden costs — the ones that unbalance my bank balance?

The amount of money needed depends on what kind of traveler you are; if you want a reasonably accurate estimate of costs, you have to be honest with yourself. After speaking with friends who had traveled to Malaysia only a few months before my own trip, I thought I would find comfortable accommodation plus good food for very little money, around $15 a day. In fact, I found that comfortable accommodation cost at least $15 a night, plus I spent about $10 a day on reliable restaurant food. I soon realized I had not budgeted enough for the kind of amenities I required. I did not sleep on the floor of backpacker's cabins nor did I eat food from street vendors. Malaysia, like many other places in the world, is a relatively cheap country in which to travel if you stay away from the cities, but one must be aware of one's needs in order to realistically estimate costs, regardless of the country. When talking with fellow travelers, ask questions to discern their needs compared to yours.

Once you determine what kind of comfort you require, you can play detective to ascertain approximate costs. Guidebooks are often not accurate in terms of estimated prices, but they can provide ballpark figures to use when planning a budget. Travel agents are another source of approximate prices and general information. If you want a fairly accurate "guess," you need to spend time in the library discovering up-to-date facts about the economy and infrastructures of a particular country. If, as in areas of Africa and South America, modern telecommunications and road systems exist only marginally, middle-priced travel is going to be more costly than in more developed Asian countries. Western European countries that have high standards of living and equally high levels of taxation are going to be expensive in every respect.

When researching costs, include accommodation, food, transportation, and entertainment, and calculate the total on a daily basis. For example, an average of $15 a night for hotels, $10 for daily food and drink, $10 for transportation, and $5 for entertainment, gives an idea of cost for the basics. Then the extras creep in. Obviously, souvenir shopping is an individual item and not included in a basic budget, but other expenses, such as a $5 book to read on tomorrow's ten-hour train ride should be budgeted beforehand.

Tongans preparing umu *local feast*

Too many extras can spoil the fun, but not budgeting enough before you leave can make the trip hardly worthwhile. If you can't experience a native feast in Tonga because it is more expensive than you had planned, one of the main reasons for the trip is defeated. Being flexible and realistic before you go will eliminate a lot of stress while traveling. If you must see Paris again before you die, accept the fact that this magical but expensive city will cost between $100 and $150 a day. Perhaps you can go for only three days — then travel by train to Chartes to relax in a *chambre d'hôte* for one third the price of a Paris hotel room, and enjoy a glass of wine in the afternoon shadows of a magnificent cathedral.

As the methods for obtaining money while traveling vary from country to country, a basic understanding of international banking is essential. See the chapter, "Money Matters" (page 106) for an explanation of ATMs (automatic teller machines) and the use of credit cards. How one gets money depends on the length and scope of the trip — a four-week sojourn in Italy can be financed before leaving with enough traveler's checks to cover most costs, plus credit cards to supplement along the way; a year going around the world requires very different strategies. Daily budget planning for each country becomes essential — you will have to have some idea of what expenses are going to be, make arrangements for a continuous supply of money from your home bank, and determine how to get the money while you are traveling. Without a doubt, the safest and most reliable way of acquiring local cash is to carry traveler's checks. And one of the easiest ways of buying traveler's checks as you go is to become a member of American Express. You have to pay of course, but an American Express Gold Card for long-term travel has many advantages: It allows you to receive mail at American Express central offices at no charge; it provides for instant replacement from a central office of a lost or stolen card; it allows you to write a personal check (for $5,000 every twenty-one days in Canada and elsewhere, every seven days in the US) on your home bank in exchange for traveler's checks (usually paying a minimal commission, depending on the country) which you will usually buy in US currency because it is the most widely accepted money in developing countries (Canadians will be paying an extra exchange rate but buying with US money almost evens the score); AMEX also offers travel services such as reservations for hotels, flights, and tours, plus rental car and other travel insurance.

Buying traveler's checks as you go is the easiest way to finance long-term travel, but planning is essential as checks can only be purchased in major centers; American Express will identify their offices around the world for you before you leave. Most other credit cards allow cash advances at major banks; you can then buy traveler's checks, but you will pay a cash advance fee on the credit card, interest on the credit card cash advance charges, plus probably a commission to buy the traveler's checks. There are limits on cash advances, so check the fine print. See "Money Matters" (page 105) for more on credit cards. If you're visiting several countries in Asia or Africa make sure you have enough US dollar traveler's checks before you leave a major center. Nairobi, Kenya has international banking; Arush, Tanzania does not. Penang, Malaysia will not cash British pound sterling or Canadian dollar traveler's checks without a hassle. Many US travelers to Israel do not exchange their US dollars for shekels as many merchants prefer to be paid with US dollars. Every country has its own idiosyncrasies, but the fact remains that the most widely accepted currency in the most out-of-the-way places is American dollars.

If you are visiting countries where you will be relying on paying by credit card, remember that the exchange rate on your credit purchase is calculated the day the charge is processed in the card company's home office. I used my Visa once in Tanzania — I was rushing to catch a bus and wanted to purchase my one-and-only souvenir from a hotel gift shop that displayed a Visa sign on the door — and the charge didn't come through for four months. Budgeting for exchange rates can sometimes make or break a journey — don't forget that extra 30 to 40 percent exchange rate tacked onto Canadian from US dollars. When Canadians use credit cards for a straight Canadian dollar exchange, they will be saving, of course. Don't forget to allow for exchange rates no matter which currency you're using, and don't forget that credit card exchanges calculated several weeks (or more) after the day of your purchase could be quite different from the date of purchase, especially if money markets are fluctuating widely as they currently are in Mexico for example.

Hidden costs lurk everywhere: unexpected tips (primarily to tour guides), insurance packages, tourist visa charges, airport departure taxes and port-of-entry fees, emergency dental bills, even the legal fees for power-of-attorney before you leave home. Most of these costs aren't actually hidden, but they either don't get included up front or they change drastically from original expectations. Tourist visas are a good example; when I visited Nepal, the $20 (US) visa fee I was quoted before leaving had been doubled four months earlier. When I entered Turkey in 1994, I was greeted with a $10 entry charge which appeared to be more like a port tax. In 1995, Americans and Canadians entering Turkey paid a visitor's fee of $20 at all border crossings. Almost any visa purchased before entering a country charges more for same-day service, so if you can't stay an extra day or two for the usual processing, same-day service can be a significant hidden cost. If driving in Europe, car entry taxes into different countries can be significant, as can toll charges on the super highways, especially in France and Italy. Airport shuttles can sneak away with a fair amount of cash, as can surprise taxi rides because the buses aren't running. Plan for extras if you are traveling either by rental car or public transportation.

If I were planning another round-the-world trip (traveling at least six months), I would calculate at least $500 for "extras" before going: medications (antimalarials are expensive), immunizations, travel cancellation insurance (for air and tour tickets), visa fees and extra passport photos.

Some unplanned expenses you're likely to encounter as you go: credit card cash advance and interest fees, medical care paid in cash for later reimbursement, camera or other equipment repair, replacing lost or stolen items and buying appropriate clothes for unexpected climate changes (if you're really cold in the Himalayas, you'll covet that $20 Tibetan wool jacket hanging in the hotel shop window in Kathmandu!).

Read the fine print of any travel medical and car rental insurance policies for extras; maybe you need to cancel and find another policy before you leave. Diligence rewards, but there will always be a surprise or two. Allow for some "free money" when planning.

Adjusting our rose-colored glasses

In 1993 nine hundred million people claimed India as their homeland, with continuous population growth projected at one million a month. In two years India's population will change by about as many people as are in Canada, or the total population of Los Angeles. This rapid transformation will affect the country's economy, its politics, the food supply, all transportation systems, even its landscape. If you backpacked in India thirty years ago, you were possibly captivated by painted elephants and plodding camel trains, charmed on houseboats on the lakes of Kashmir, and awed before elaborate burning pyres on the sacred Ganges. When you

Preparing for cremation, Bali

travel in India today, you will still be fascinated by painted elephants and camel trains transporting goods, although you may not be able to travel in Kashmir because of political unrest and you will be aware that only cremations of the rich are carried out with colorful ceremony. Ultraviolet rays stabbing through depleted ozone layers over India in the 1990s are so fierce that the rosy-hued sunglasses of the 1960s have been replaced by eye-protecting shades of blue or black. Modern India not only requires sunglasses of a different color; it also demands that travelers' romantic expectations and recollections be tempered with reality.

We are older, and we know that the world is changing at breakneck speed. It would have been best to have visited Bali ten or even twenty years ago, before the invasion of tourists and the inevitable inroads into the unique local culture. However, today many Balinese tenaciously cling to their traditions, and Bali is still worth a visit. Pick a time that is off-season (definitely not over Christmas holidays) and venture into the rice paddies where it is still possible to stay in luxury accommodation for $40 a night and watch flocks of white herons skim overhead in early

Not quite wild, Camp Leakey, Indonesia

morning light. Don't miss seeing the Taj Mahal because of frightening tales of beggars in India; they aren't allowed inside the fenced grounds — and the Taj truly is an architectural wonder of the world.

For the most part, as seniors, we have an understanding and tolerance gained with our years, but when we travel, these are put to the test. Our mature patience will reap its rewards if we don't allow ourselves to get too tired and become irritated by petty requests. I almost caused an international incident in the bus depot in Tel Aviv when I was refused entrance to the public washroom because I didn't have the proper coin the attendant demanded I pay. When I tried to enter without paying, the shouting of the madame created such a ruckus I was forced to abandon my mission. I was momentarily very angry, until I realized I was really very tired. I simply couldn't cope with what I thought at the time was an outrageous demand.

Disappointment won't happen if we adjust our expectations. Independent travel always includes surprises. The adventure is in the unknown, although if one isn't prepared for discovery, travel can turn into torture. The value of research before planning cannot be overstated. Borrow several different guidebooks of the same area and read the preambles about history, geography, religion, political structures, food, and industry. Try to talk to someone who has been there. Ask specific questions to see how much they actually contacted local people, what kind of accommodation they used, where they ate and how they got around.

Accounts by travel writers give the authors' personal interpretations of trips including everything from exotic mountain climbing and jungle explorations to historic sites in the city where you were born. Check resource files at the library for accounts of encounters with orangutans in Borneo or the hill tribe aborigines of Northern Thailand if you're planning an adventure to these areas. There probably isn't any spot on earth that hasn't been invaded and written about by someone from the "outside," including Irian Jaya, Indonesia with its recently discovered headhunting tribes. Research takes time, but it will enhance your trip.

Chapter Two

Encounters

One on one with the natives, or how to say hello

In Italy a cheery *ciao* brings response any time of the day; in France you may tip your hat with *bonjour* until six o'clock in the evening and then switch to *bonsoir*; in Nepal friendly natives sing *namaste* as they pass you on the trail; in Turkey *merhaba* is often answered with an English hello. After I had been in India for ten days, I realized I hadn't learned their customary greeting because English is spoken when dealing with tourists whom most local people ignore, especially in areas of high tourist traffic.

Avoiding locals who are jaded by tourism can be a challenge, but forays off the beaten track can reveal such a variety of people that one wonders if one is still in the same country. While pick-pockets and every kind of thievery are normal on the coastal tourist routes of Mexico, visits to small colonial cities of the central plateau do not pose threats to one's security that require more than ordinary safety measures. You can relax while you chat

Muslims and Buddhas in the eye of the camera

with school children who want to hear your English and who hopefully will trade responses in Spanish. Often it is the exuberance of young people that overcomes the shyness of their elders. Learning the basics — hello, goodbye, please, thank you, what is your name? — will open doors into foreign worlds and into our own. The curiosity is mutual.

As visitors, we become ambassadors for our country — a window into another world — and as seniors we are often more approachable than younger travelers. When I climbed several hundred steps to the top of the largest Buddhist monument in the world at Borobodur on Java, Indonesia, I was surrounded by groups of Muslim teenagers who wanted to know my name, how old I was, where I lived. Conversation led to photo sessions, mainly with veiled young women who wanted to identify with English-speaking visitors, but also with young men who arranged themselves around the Buddhist Stupas in Western-style poses — like the models they have seen in foreign magazines. We all laughed when I tried to convince the school kids that I was not a model posing for their shots, and I didn't require that they pose.

Unfortunately, in many places of the world, cameras signify a kind of profiteering. Mothers in the hills of Thailand have learned to place their youngsters under the village standpipe for a timely "country bath" and then ask for money when passing trekkers click their shutters to capture the native scene. Be aware of these "opportunities" — sometimes they are craftily hidden — and keep your lens cap screwed in place. Being a voyeur and exploiting the natives is not the role of interested travelers attempting to understand another culture.

In some countries, local people are eager to explain their customs to foreigners. Turks are always ready for a glass of tea, and in small villages, the more adventurous will invite you to their homes. Children are often intermediaries; young Maasai want to show their cool, mud and stick igloo-shaped houses while their mothers stay in the village center to display beadwork and hope for a sale. In Fiji we were invited to visit a village school to tell where we were from, what kind of work we did (we avoided "retirement"), and what our house looked like. Luckily the two sets of felt pens I had brought from home were enough for each student to have one. The problem of no paper on which to draw was hopefully going to be solved by the teacher the next day.

Giving small tokens of friendship can create chaos if there isn't enough for each person to have their own. Balloons and felt pens are lightweight, easy to pack, and stretch around a group of children, but they need to be dispensed individually. If you are with a guide, consult with him before giving gifts. They may advise a different time or place for your benevolence. I had great fun with small hard bouncing balls when there were just a few young children — two or three are manageable, but not five or six. Lapel stick pins of your native flag are handy to give to guides or anyone who shows interest in your homeland, especially when it's photo time.

It needs to be said that many areas have suffered invasion by denigrating tourists who think it's great sport to throw token coins at natives or tease children into begging for a gift. One story our African guide related was of white tourists who dangled pens behind their slowly moving truck in order to get native children to chase them. Now children run after safari vehicles yelling "give me pen" repeatedly — or the more unfriendly tribes

Making friends, Thai hill tribes

shoot unwelcome campers with deadly poisoned arrows (a Canadian on safari died in 1994). Need we wonder why?

Gifts are not necessary, but learning to say hello in the local language is a must if you want to feel comfortable in a strange environment. No one expects you to carry on a conversation in Swahili or Bahassa Indonesian or even French. However, the back roads of France can be more difficult than the Maasai steppes because most French will not speak English whereas Africans want to try to understand you. If you are in a country that requires that you learn their language, you have no choice but to tote a phrase book and dictionary at all times. This will come in handy wherever you are; they are readily available in major European languages, but may be more difficult to obtain for Brazilian Portuguese or Israeli Hebrew. Berlitz and Cortina are two popular lines of language travel books. Consult your local travel bookseller for mail order information.

Backpacking seniors: independence on a learning curve

When traveling, the world becomes a hands-on event. Television, E-mail, the Internet, and library loans are left at home. Perspectives shift as new environments force us to become active participants rather than passive observers. At last it's the real thing. It is thrilling to be part of a live audience as marching soldiers in *Aida* progress triumphantly upstage at Australia's world-famous Sydney Opera House. Following the opera, when we perch high on the top steps of that dazzling landmark, mesmerized by boating lights and ferry happenings on Sydney Harbour, we know our view is not television. Neither is it a painting, and it's never static. The entire evening's experience has been unique to us.

Whether climbing aboard cantankerous elephants for a trek in Thailand or risking terrorist bombs in the Grand Bazaar of Istanbul, our actions can be puzzling to non-travelers — those not bitten by the traveling bug. But for those of us who perch ourselves on the learning curve of the world, these diverse experiences are essential to our well-being. Armchair traveling does not satisfy our curiosity nor our quest for adventure.

Independence on too steep a learning curve can be frightening or even dangerous. Before ascending that elephant-boarding platform, you need to know that you are expected to grip a shallow board saddle for two hours of sun-drenched mountain climbing, elephant style. Since there is no way of getting off the elephant before the ultimate destination is reached, you need to know your personal limitations. Can you last for two hours? What if the ride stretches to three hours? Being aware of one's abilities is one side of the equation; understanding what is required by the situation is the other side. It is not always easy to determine what a trek or elephant ride involves, but talking with a guide or tour operator and stating one's concerns helps. Keep in mind that a stranger's thirst for business can produce misleading "guarantees"; for best results, talk to a fellow traveler who has just returned from the same expedition you are contemplating.

Climbing aboard, elephant trekking in Thailand

Elderhostel (see "Appendix D" for address) is an organization that is forthright in stating its expectations; their 1996 Antarctica tour advertisement clearly says in bold letters that the program requires participants to be "physically fit and vigorous." Some expedition/trekking companies make hiking to the 19,340 foot summit of Mt. Kilimanjaro sound like a Sunday stroll. Question both of these types of opportunities before you make your deposit. Organizations should give more information when pressed; if they refuse, find another company.

No matter how you travel (with a group or on your own), in-depth investigation before you leave home cannot be avoided. You need to know what equipment is required. How many hours are in a day's hike? Are boating procedures safe? Does the river rafting company provide life preservers? What about stormy weather — what are normal temperatures and conditions? What do you need to know about food, meals, drinking water? What are the costs of transportation and how easy is it to obtain? How much is a guide? Are you expected to hire a porter? What medical facilities are available, especially for altitude sickness if your destination is above ten thousand feet? What permits are required? Where will you sleep?

After your research is complete, the most important question remains: Are you physically capable of accomplishing what you want to do? Be honest with your answer! Backpacking with a full load over rough terrain for five days may be better left to the younger at heart — and body. There probably is a similar experience awaiting you on a more accessible trail.

We all like the idea of traveling independently, but there are times when joining a small group is not only easier physically but reassuring for security reasons. My husband and I trekked for four days in Nepal with a local guide and porters hired through a tour operator in Kathmandu. We were the only people in our party. Our guide gave us careful instructions for attaching our packs to our tent support pole and keeping our cameras and money belts inside our sleeping bags while we slept, as tents are sometimes skillfully cut and belongings stolen. I was very happy, later in the evening, to have another group of campers join us at the campsite. The sounds of our English mixed with their Norwegian plus the Nepalese bantering of the guides and porters created a guarded camaraderie nine thousand feet into the foothills of the Himalayas.

Basic survival depends on communication. If you are not comfortable with requesting a beer in a foreign language, and you really have to sip a foaming pint at the end of a long day, perhaps you need to confine your travels to English-speaking countries. Ventures into more remote corners of the world require that one pay attention constantly. This is tiring — and stressful — and requires plenty of time to rest and recover both your physical and mental faculties. When renting a car in strange territory, arrange for pickup after you've acclimatized to the area. Stay a few nights at a neighbourhood hotel before attempting to cope with unintelligible road signs (also driving on the left and getting around the roundabouts if these are new to you) as well as the initial verbal mishmash of a foreign tongue. Communicating in a language different from our own hones listening skills, most importantly when we are seeking directions. Confusion can often occur if we've become so involved with asking the question that we've forgotten to concentrate on the answer!

If your learning curve has been climbing too sharply, relaxing with a glass of local brew can save the day. Beer's two greatest virtues are that it's usually cheap, and it's safe to drink! It appears almost without bidding (except in Muslim countries). Universally, the sound of the word is familiar — *bir, birah, bier, bière, birra* — Spanish *cerveza* is an exception. Even if you don't usually drink beer at home, you run the risk of becoming a worldly connoisseur if you start comparing foreign pints. Was Nepalese beer stronger than Indian brew, or the Greek version tastier than Turkish? Just be careful to not bestow your Indian accolades on the Nepalese, or confuse Greeks with Turks — your local drinking partners may lose their agreeable smiles!

National drinks can be interesting as well as inexpensive. Don't visit France without trying the popular apéritif pastis, or Greece without at least one round of ouzo accompanied by snake dancing to strumming bouzoukis. A $4 quart bottle of Turkish raki, similar in anise flavour to ouzo and pastis, disappears surprisingly quickly. I've sipped some wonderful sour rice wine on Bali and some awful rice plonk in Thailand.

Solo travel: pros and cons

To go alone or stay at home — that is the question. And there are a million answers, both pro and con. Which solution is appropriate for you depends on a multitude of factors.

Since a lot depends on where, when, and how you're going, gather these facts together first. Then try to get a firm grip on your objectives. Are you traveling to see a country, to meet people, to learn a language, to research a book, to take photographs, to test your courage, or just to know you've been there? Probably your answers include some or maybe even all of the above.

If you're contemplating riding your bike around the world next year, or climbing every reasonably large mountain in the Southern Hemisphere before 2001, you won't be reading this section. You've already decided to take the risks. But if risk taking is still uppermost on your list of concerns, you need to seriously consider your objectives along with an appraisal of your traveling personality. Are you easily intimidated? Do you usually rely on someone else to communicate for you in a foreign language? How flexible can you be, both physically and emotionally? Can you interpret maps and get across London on the underground by yourself? Can you manage all those strange currencies and exchange rates? Are you demanding or do you have the patience of Job? How much do you need to be alone or to have company?

If you are a solo woman heading for the more raucous Mediterranean countries known for flirtatious men or for Muslim populations where men view foreign females as part of their free enterprise system, be prepared for hassle. If you decide this isn't your cup of tea, choose another country or take a partner with you. Two women traveling in Turkey can have a fabulous vacation; one woman on her own will miss a lot when she is forced to stay within the protection of popular tourist sites in daylight hours. There are several good books for women traveling alone; consult your library or travel bookstore (see "Appendix A" for a recommended title).

Some parts of Central and South America are dangerous for anyone traveling on their own. Belize City is billed as a retirement haven for North Americans but after dark the downtown streets are a no man's land of crime. While visiting aboard a sailing yacht anchored off the main pier, a female crew member and the captain got their signals crossed about the time she was to return to the boat from a trip inland. They didn't connect, and when the captain finally went to the police in the early evening to file a missing person report, he was a victim of an attempted mugging. Meanwhile, the crew member found her own way out to the boat just before dark. Needless to say, a happy reunion was had by all once they had returned unscathed, but there were firm orders from the skipper for everyone to remain on the boat at night.

While security problems pose a deterrent to traveling alone in some areas, not everywhere in the world is unsafe for solo travelers. If you are a gregarious person, eager to communicate in any language, and do not make unyielding demands on your-

Kho Phi Phi R&R, Thailand

self as well as others, you can enjoy figuring out how to pay for your own coffee before you find a seat in a village square for the local band concert. And if you want company for the concert, you are sure to find it where you are staying or at other backpacker's "hangouts." Word gets around, people meet people ... and you may much prefer this way of traveling to being saddled with a partner who insists on five-star accommodation that is not only too expensive for your budget, but insulates both of you from the culture you are trying to experience.

There are probably fewer seniors traveling alone than the younger generation, but sharing experiences and travel tips occurs regardless of age. I have been flattered by backpackers my children's age who, when we have been comparing notes, have allowed that "my parents would never travel like you're doing," meaning traveling independently and learning from fellow travelers. It's true that I choose to not go alone because I find that mediating the stress of independent travel with a partner makes the trip more enjoyable for me; but I know that the freedom of being responsible just for oneself can be exhilarating, and everything from European alpine chalets to South Pacific beach bungalows are waiting to occupy days or even weeks of solitude. However, the old axioms of "never hike alone" and "never swim alone" cannot be repeated too often. Whether we want to admit it or not, broken bones and rushing river currents become more difficult as we get older.

A three-week trek on the Coast to Coast Walk in England is very different from the same distance and time covered on the Annapurna Circuit in Nepal. In England you don't hire a guide (or porter), you don't have to think about altitude sickness, the food is familiar, and the most you have to worry about is how much it might rain. In Nepal the trail may be blocked by an avalanche, or you might have to be rushed down a 14,000 foot (4,200m) mountain pass because you're vomiting, disoriented, short of breath, and nursing a pounding headache. When you recover from the altitude sickness, you may not be able to tolerate the local diet of daal bhaat washed down with chang. You may even dream about tea and raisin scones before a cheery fire in an English cottage in the Yorkshire Dales where you wouldn't have the fabulous Annapurna Himal towering above you. In England you would be comfortable with the language and food, security would be less of a challenge, and you would have a greater chance of staying healthy, but the thrill of adventure would be tempered by familiarity. And you can twist your ankle anywhere.

Cost is definitely a factor when making your decision; obtaining an accurate picture is essential if operating on a tight budget. Even if you have considerable financial leeway, you need to know how much money to take with you into the hinterlands. Sometimes it is cheaper to go on your own; sometimes it is less expensive with a group. If you want to do a private safari in East Africa, you must hire a vehicle and guide (Tanzania game parks will not allow you to travel on your own and you are not permitted to walk in lion country), both of which are more costly than attaching yourself to a small group. To give a further idea of

Roughing it on the Serengeti Plain, Tanzania

expense, every camper in Serengeti National Park pays $20 per night to camp plus a $20 entry fee into the park, regardless of how they are traveling. Adding private transportation and guides on top of these basics makes watching "the big five" grazing in their natural habitat a very expensive proposition.

All of these factors determine how you will go. If you are single and looking for a partner, there are many opportunities sprouting in travel newsletters. *International Living* runs a column of ads for "Travelers seeking travelers" as does *Cast Travel News* (see "Appendix A" for addresses). Check your local newspaper — that's how my husband met our first cycling companions for France whom we've now been cycling with for several years.

If you go solo, know your limitations. Don't overtax yourself, so you can stay healthy and happy. If you travel with a partner, your choices of where and how you go will broaden; if you travel with a group, you may face some restrictions of flexibility but increased security can be a major plus. However you go, dedicate your travel journals to someone you trust. Who knows? Someday they may be published.

Chapter Three

Planning

Agents, accreditations, and rapport

Establishing a working relationship with a travel agent can be one of the most important aspects of your trip. You cannot avoid working with an agent if you want to purchase the best airfares available. Buying direct from an airline does allow you to purchase their ultra super saver and APEX (advance purchase excursion) fares, but because the airline's restrictions on advance purchases and their cancellation penalties can be quite complicated, it is imperative that you understand all the rules and regulations. A qualified agent is the best person to interpret these kinds of fares for you, plus introduce you to the myriad other special fares available. An individual does not have access to the particulars of an agent's data base. Even if you are able to tap into computer travel sources, full disclosure of restrictions and notices of current specials are not always posted. A recent travel statistic claims that airlines make over 50,000 changes *a day* to their fare structures.

And now that deregulation has allowed airlines to contract ticket sales to wholesalers who in turn sell to travel agents — in contrast to the old commission system — an agent becomes a necessity if you want to purchase the lowest fare available.

Your primary objective is to get an agent to understand your needs. If you want the cheapest fare, regardless of time or day or week, say so. If your agent provides you with only one choice, ask for quotes from all the airlines that fly to your destination and not just the one ticketed by the agent's brother-in-law.

Regardless of whom you choose to do business with — whether it's a mass purchaser such as a consolidator specializing in discount fares or a general travel agent — you must have someone with whom you can communicate with ease and who is readily available by phone. Dealing with someone who is especially tuned in to seniors' discounts also helps.

Look for notices of accreditation and bonding; qualified agents display their certificates on their office walls and initials of accreditation on their letterheads and business cards. Canadian accredited agencies are members of the Alliance of Canadian Travel Associates (ACTA) and the International Air Transport Association (IATA). IATA certifies agencies world-wide. American agencies are accredited by the International Airlines Travel Agent Network (IATAN) and the Airlines Reporting Corporation (ARC). In Canada, the Bank Settlement Plan (BSP) is a clearing facility that collects money from agents and distributes it to the proper airlines; in the US, ARC has a similar function. Both BSP and ARC provide money settlement plans to agents and both have stringent membership requirements. While most of these accrediting organizations are connected with airlines, other participants in the travel industry such as cruise operators, hotels, and car rental companies will not pay commissions unless they recognize the major airline credentials behind an agency.

Individual states (California, Hawaii, Illinois, Ohio, Rhode Island, Washington, Iowa, Florida, and Oregon in 1993) and provinces (British Columbia, Ontario, and Quebec) have passed legislation protecting consumers by setting up assurance funds for bankruptcy refunds of an airline, tour operator or agency. One of the best protection devises for consumers anywhere in the US or Canada is to pay with a credit card and get a receipt; in fact most travel advisors say to always pay with a credit card because it has its own bankruptcy protection. Another reassurance suggestion is to check hotels listed in a tour package for reservations under the tour company's name. Also, ask the company about their own liability clauses and coverage for their errors or omissions. Membership in the National Tour Association (NTA, see "Appendix E" for address) includes $1,000,000 liability insurance and "proof of good track record." Dealing with a company that has been in business long enough to establish a good track record will provide recommendations and testimonies of good service. Of course these comments are subject to individual interpretation, but longevity itself is an indication of dependability.

The British Columbia Travel Agent Act is noted for its careful protection of the consumer. The American Society of Travel Agents (ASTA) runs a highly respected Consumer Affairs Department (see "Appendix E" for address) where consumers can file complaints and check on complaints previously reported. Local Better Business Bureaus are another source for verification of viable business practices of your local agency. The Better Business Bureau of Metropolitan New York has published a *Ticket Consolidator Advisory Report* available from 257 Park Avenue South, New York 10010, New York, USA.

In today's world of mass discount travel by massive numbers of travelers, it has become acceptable for airlines to sell large volumes of tickets to consolidators or wholesalers who then sell to agents for higher commissions than airlines pay. If you are purchasing tickets from an insured registered discount agent, you have a reasonable guarantee that all tickets — used or unused — will be honored. Accreditation also *usually* guarantees that if a registered agency ceases to operate as a business, moneys deposited on tours or tickets will be refunded. Another point to consider is that if you have unsuccessfully tried a holiday special offered

Windjammer cruising off Pangkor Island, Malaysia

through an accredited agency, you possibly will have some recourse if your experience has turned out to be less than advertised.

How agents operate and get paid is a constantly changing scene. The current news is that airlines have placed a ceiling on how much commission will be paid to agencies, so most tickets are now purchased from wholesalers who pay commissions directly to agents. The bottom line is that you, the consumer, pay no obvious fee to an agent who may spend hours routing your around-the-world itinerary — unless you deal with a travel consultant who may charge as much as $35 an hour to get you where you want to go, sometimes at a considerable saving. Paying a fee to someone who will take the time to construct a customised package for your travel requirements is money well spent. You will not be rushed out the door because an agent needs to sell more tickets that day in order to fill his or her commission quota, and you will not be charged "overrides" or hidden fees tacked on to your discount ticket fare.

Planning an in-depth tour to one or two out-of-the-way places may require an agent who specializes in your destination. While large chains of agencies can tap into a flood of global travel facts, smaller speciality agents who limit their knowledge to a specific area can zero in on your particular interests. Because they are familiar with the local scene — they are either from there or have spent time exploring the region — they can provide answers to such concerns as climate variations and security measures. Also, they likely have access to the cheapest local transportation rates. Consult an agency for oriental holidays if you want to explore Indonesia. If heading for Patagonia and Tierra del Fuego, a Caribbean cruise specialist would not be an agent of choice.

"CTC" after a travel agent's name means he or she has taken courses to become a Certified Travel Counsellor. These courses, given by the Institute of Certified Travel Agents (ICTA), provide destination knowledge to travel agents. One of the attractions of the travel agency business has always been the travel perks supplied to agents, and according to some, these perks are increasing. As a whole, the tourist industry is recognizing the value of hands-on experience that gets passed on to consumers. If you want to know what a weekend at the Hyatt's latest colossal resort complex on Maui would be like, chances are someone in the office has been there on a promotion package. Destinations such as Thailand and Malaysia are strongly promoting tourism so there is a good chance someone has also visited tiny Pangkor Island off the west coast of Malaysia.

Planning extended travel that involves several countries cannot be accomplished without change; itineraries have to be flexible in the beginning stages because airline schedules as well as political and personal factors move dates and times. If you're working with an agent who has difficulty with making changes to suit your needs or who vacillates on the phone or doesn't return your calls, scout around for a replacement. Discovering a friendly, competent agent can be like finding a national treasure — if you really can communicate, and he or she really is willing to wade through your changes and uncertainties, treat them with kindness and respect.

Dealing with scarce information and reservations for vague dates requires perseverance on their part as well as your own. An agent may well choose to not bother with you. My traveling partner and I had difficulty getting agents to work with us as soon as they realized we were customizing our round-the-world

Holy day at the Wailing Wall, Jerusalem, Israel

itinerary because established air routes did not fit our requirements. We approached our tried-and-true agent in the small city where we used to live, and when he didn't return our calls, it became obvious that we had to look elsewhere. After again getting no response in a larger center crawling with agencies, we tried in the small town near where we now live and unexpectedly found our treasure.

Whether your aim is to get all the way around the world or to a single small island in the Mediterranean, keep careful notes and a separate calendar to organize payment schedules, deadlines, and reservations. Don't rely on your agent to remember to book an air or inter-island ferry pass for somewhere you mentioned three months ago and then forgot about; most likely he or she will have forgotten also, and you will find at the last minute the pass has not been purchased. Keeping accurate notes in an up-to-date file is as much your responsibility as your agent's.

When booking anything — transportation, accommodation, or a tour — you may be asked to sign a disclaimer that includes anything from a 100 percent nonrefundable clause to no changes allowed. Be sure that you understand what you are signing before you put your signature on the dotted line. It is not uncommon for tour companies to offer their insurance to cover their tour along with a disclaimer notice for you to sign and return if you decline their terms. This you would do if you find their offer duplicates insurance you already have; for example, trip cancellation and personal property coverage.

If you sign the form waiving the tour company's insurance, it simply lets them off the hook and makes you responsible for collecting payment from your own insurance if you have to cancel or your suitcase gets left behind. It is easy to get trapped into duplicate insurances. Check your home owner's policy and credit card coverage before you sign for unnecessary extras, or for not enough in the case of disclaimers. For more on insurance see "Security: Guarantees and Insurances," page 70.

Open booking versus fixed dates

One certainty with visiting a foreign country is that you must enter and then leave. Deciding when to come and go depends upon tour arrangements and personal obligations. If one has reserved a two-week safari to begin and end on specific dates, entry and departure times are decided before leaving home. If seeing a country is entirely dependent on whatever happens to appear on the horizon after one has arrived, timing becomes a matter of personal preference — until departure day.

Many travelers like the idea of "no fixed date;" an open-ended ticket is their dream of independence. But they haven't considered the two or three days necessary to stay near a travel agent, train or bus station, boat dock, or airport while making arrangements to exit a country. Their independence runs the risk of being a costly sacrifice while they wait for a connection to their next destination. Maybe that connection happens only on Saturdays, and their initial inquiry began on Monday because they were confident they would be accommodated during off-peak weekdays. Now there isn't any choice but to hang around a port-of-entry (or exit) until the weekend.

Open-ended travel is costly in more ways than one. Not only might you have the added expense of accommodation and food while waiting (especially if this is non-productive travel time), but you may be paying a higher fare than if you had purchased a discount ticket before leaving home. Added to the intrigue of actual ticket buying are the aspects of currency exchange and foreign language transactions. Can you be sure that even though the ticket agent speaks English, he or she hasn't padded their pocket at your expense? Keeping track of exchange rates and real value of a fare in your money is difficult under ideal circumstances; misunderstanding and miscalculations in a foreign office present challenges that are frustrating as well as time consuming. If you are forced to complete transactions in Greek or Thai or Portuguese, will you feel your heart sink when you watch the take-off of a half empty plane on which you would have had a seat if you could have communicated more effectively?

While the disadvantages of open-ended travel can be hidden, the absolutes of fixed dates are obvious. Since departure dates and times are known, explorations are planned with this in mind. There is no guessing involved and no hassle to secure passage on overbooked or unreliable transports. Prepayment has been taken care of and you don't have to find cash or try to deal with a ticket agent on a weekend or holiday when banks are closed. If an unforeseen delay presents itself, it is usually possible to change your pre-bought ticket, perhaps paying a small penalty.

Most six months to a year around-the-world air fares require a fixed departure date only on the first international leg of the your expedition. After the initial flight, you are on your own to

Hiking Franz Josef Glacier, New Zealand

enjoy flexibility. Your only responsibility is to hop the next available flight when you choose to leave a country. However, if you are flying out of a major international terminal, this could involve a few days' wait, or you may be forced to accept awkward times. If connecting with smaller carriers for a planned but not booked side trip, you may have a long wait to get a seat on a heavily used weekly local flight.

Around-the-world carriers stipulate that tickets be purchased from fourteen to twenty-one days prior to departure. This allows quite a lot of freedom for a traveler to make last minute plans. You can purchase a ticket and be on your way two weeks later. This may be a significant factor if you want to pay for the ticket just before leaving. Cancellation policies include anything from 10 to 25 percent penalties for cancelling within specified periods of time. Changes and stopover conditions vary also, but usually itinerary changes or rerouting are permitted free of charge one time only. There are also restrictions on traveling from one hemisphere to another, and of course one must travel continuously eastward or continuously westward and there is no backtracking.

All of these rules and regulations mean careful scrutiny of the fine print. The fares are certainly attractive — especially any upgrade from economy class — but you will probably do better on your own with careful shopping. When I planned my around-the-world eight-month adventure, I had to purchase from a consolidator because my first port-of-call was in the South Pacific. I then made my way across New Zealand, Australia and Southeast Asia; traveled as far north as Nepal; stopped in Delhi; detoured down to Tanzania in East Africa and finally came to rest in the Middle East and Turkey. While airline's fixed southern or northern hemisphere routings do not strictly adhere to one hemisphere or another, if one wants to mix and match as much as I did, it's not possible to use a pre-established fare.

I fixed my schedule before leaving home and had no difficulty changing flights out of Nairobi to Tel Aviv rather than Cairo when I learned in Africa that my prebooked Nile cruise had been cancelled and that the American embassy had temporarily evacuated their quarters in Cairo because of terrorist bombings. In hindsight, the change of scene from Egypt to Israel wasn't a whole lot more secure, but no catastrophes arose out of the Negev while I was in close proximity.

Only my final flight from Europe to North America was left open on my itinerary. After spending two days with a travel agent on Rhodes, Greece (plus long distance calls from Turkey to London) to arrange a flight home after eight months of travel, I gained a full appreciation for the convenience of prebooking. I was able to purchase a less expensive London-Vancouver ticket from a bucket shop outside London than if I had booked eight or more months earlier (which is why I waited), but the whole procedure was time-consuming and tedious. The fact that relatives in England received my ticket voucher for me in the mail plus accommodated me on my stop-over greatly facilitated obtaining the ticket, and also helped to ease my return to the real world.

If you do your homework and construct tentative itineraries for the countries you want to visit, an entire trip can be prebooked. And if you buy tickets from an accredited agent, you can be assured of refunds for any unused portion. Granted, a round-the-world open ticket from an airline isn't entirely unstructured because your routing has been predetermined, but you still have the possibility of wasting precious travel time if you can't get on a desired flight, especially during peak travel times.

It's handy to know about *OAG Desktop Flight Guide, Worldwide Edition* published monthly for the travel industry. Contained within the three-inch-thick telephone-book-size volume is everything you want to know about air travel. Its updated revisions *almost* guarantee current schedules and at the least tell you what airlines fly where. Ask your travel agent for an outdated volume, compile a list of the countries you want to visit, make a chart for approximate arrival and departure dates, and plan your holiday of a life-time.

If you are traveling by car, find out about ferry reservations and schedules and allow more than enough time to secure your spot. If you are traveling from the north to south islands of New Zealand (or south to north), don't listen to people who tell you it isn't necessary to book more than a few days before you want to cross Cook Strait, even in low season. Make the long distance call as soon as you can commit yourself to a date. Getting across the English Channel requires the same foresight; the rule of thumb is "don't wait to make your reservation." Scandinavian ferries differ slightly from country to country but they all accept reservations. Guidebooks and travel agents have access to this kind of information.

Which countries, which hemispheres: weather, climate, and time zones

When to go is a very important consideration when compiling an itinerary. The Annapurna Circuit in Nepal cannot be trekked if the trail is buried under snow, and a sailing holiday in the Caribbean is not a great idea during hurricane season. Seniors, for the most part, do not want to travel during peak tourist times so an understanding of climatic conditions in all hemispheres becomes of paramount important on the research agenda.

It is difficult to think snow when it's 80°F (26°C) in the afternoon shade of the front deck, but chances are it is snowing (or rainy and cold) in the high country of New Zealand's Milford Sound while we enjoy summer in the Northern Hemisphere, so you wouldn't plan on touring that country's Southern Alps in July (although some New Zealanders say these uncrowded times are the best for visiting, in spite of cooler temperatures, shorter days, and increased rainfall). We know that it is perpetually warm around the equator (at low elevations), but tropical monsoons and hurricanes produce months of high rain and humidity that can be avoided. Optimum weather conditions for visiting Papeete occur in August and September (contrary to when most North Americans head for the South Pacific); Singapore and Indonesia are the most comfortable during their dry season (May through September); the Caribbean's best time is late winter or early spring (December through April), after the high winds of June through November.

Study the weather section of guidebooks to determine when to go. Some places you may have a choice, as in the two dry seasons of most East African countries or Nepal. Tom Loffman and Randy Mann's *International Traveler's Weather Guide* (see "Appendix A" for mail order information), gives a broad overview of major destinations. Before planning your itinerary, take the time to research weather information. You need to know what to pack, and what to expect weather-wise if it is important to what you are hoping to see and do. You may not mind spend-

Reef watching, sailing in Tonga

ing a rainy week in the Outer Hebrides if you are working on a manuscript, but you might be too uncomfortable in Fiji's highest humidity that confines you to an air-conditioned room when you would rather be on the beach.

When a round-the-world air ticket begins with a northern hemisphere gateway and then labels itself a southern hemisphere route, it will usually take you to the South Pacific and Australia and New Zealand. You may get a side-trip to South America for a small additional fare. As of this writing, British Airways and United have a North Pacific route that includes Hong Kong; BA also teams up with Quantas and Singapore Air to allow a European plus African option before returning to Toronto or Pittsburgh. KLM and Singapore Air combine to include points in South America or Africa. Canadian Airlines joins with several carriers around the world to get you almost anywhere you want to go. Airline affiliations and routings constantly change; consult a round-the-world specialist for up-to-date airline brochures on round-the-world routes and fares.

If considering an around-the-world ticket, airlines and travel agents suggest that you begin your planning by making a list of countries you wish to visit. List in hand, plot a course between major cities, always traveling in either an easterly or westerly direction. Even if it looks like you will have a lot of add-ons or side trips, you may find a round-the-world fare that works. If you want to team up with your own frequent flyer plan, you may run into stumbling blocks. My major stumbling block was finding an airline that allowed me to begin my trip flying westerly and to the South Pacific. Almost all the around-the-world fare structures fly North America to Europe — and I definitely wanted to go the other way. And I'm very glad I did. The number one reason? No jet lag! My initial flight was five hours (Vancouver to Hawaii) in the same direction as my biological clock — I progressed into the night of the same day of departure instead of leap-frogging into the next day if I had flown towards the sun. From Hawaii I went straight south for six hours to the Cook Islands. This took most of the night, of course, but when I arrived at 8:30 A.M. after a few hours of sleep on the plane (I declined Air New Zealand's 2:00 A.M. breakfast — a serving habit of some carriers that seems impossible to alter), I was only three hours ahead of my home time. A nap in the afternoon, lulled by the surf breaking on Rarotonga's shore, was all I needed for a memorable inauguration to eight months of travel around the world. Subsequent flights of the entire trip were never more than three hours (except for six hours from Sydney, Australia to Jakarta, Indonesia and from Bombay to Nairobi), and I never suffered from jet lag.

Number two reason for going west to east and staying in the Southern Hemisphere or just north of the equator from October through February was no winter! I had continuous spring or summer for five months followed by the last of Tanzania's spring dry season in March, and finally a pre-summer warm-up on the

Aegean coast of Turkey for April and May. My visit to Indonesia (Kalimantan, Bali, Java) was during the monsoon season which was unavoidable, but it's true that the downpours are sudden, brief, and usually in the afternoon, so all one needs is a rain poncho or umbrella (a poncho is cool, packs easily, and keeps cameras and backpacks dry).

I crossed the international date line in Fiji after visiting two countries and changing my watch twice. Bang — it was the next day, and I had no physical reaction to the change. If I had flown Vancouver to London, I would have flown for nine hours and gained eight hours in time, which is tough on anybody. If you cannot avoid flying eastwards, allow at least a day for your biological clock to adjust before heading into the unknown.

Through the skies, over land, or across the water

Since government deregulation of airlines, discount tickets have acquired legal status; bucket shops and consolidators no longer suggest illicit, under-the-counter operations unless they are not accredited (by IATA, BSP, or ARC — see "Planning: Agents, accreditations, and rapport" page 35). Consumers now know that airlines routinely sell blocks of tickets to wholesalers who are able to pass savings on to the general public and at the same time pay travel agents a higher commission than the airlines pay. It's a matter of expediency; the airlines require less personnel, the mark-up is reduced, and hopefully more people are traveling at a reduced fare.

Agents who consolidate one-way tickets — for example, an around-the-world itinerary — purchase tickets from contractors who specialize in specific areas, say Southeast Asia. The agent then deals with another contractor for India, then possibly another for the Middle East and North Africa or whatever is required to complete the routing. These tickets have been purchased at a wholesale rate from the airlines and part of the savings is passed on to you, the customer. Agents also work through an organization called Air Brokers Network which supplies them with information on contractors and consolidators. In the US, most

Delicious wild herb and goat cheese crêpes, Turkey

tickets are now sold to agents through a middleman or contractor, unless an agent is specializing in arranging block bookings for corporate groups or similar tours. In that case the agent may deal directly with an airline. But when it comes to individual requests, a major airline really doesn't want to bother finding the lowest fare available from Toronto or New York to London on the first Monday of next month returning ten days later at three o'clock in the afternoon. And an agent doesn't want to spend hours in front of a computer screen seeking answers to the same question repeated to several airlines. If you, the consumer or the agent, really want the cheapest fare, you won't get it from an airline. You need to do business with a discount agency who has access to the Air Brokers Network or a similar service of contractors and consolidators who immediately tap into the block of tickets they have already purchased at a wholesale rate because they are buying in bulk. The ticketing then literally takes a matter of minutes before a voucher is issued and you are on your way.

When I purchased a return ticket from London to Vancouver from a recommended (by a Canadian travel consultant living in Greece) discount agent near London via telephone from Turkey, my initial request was confirmed within an hour and the ticket voucher mailed to a relative in England within twenty-four hours. The ticket was non-refundable so I purchased a cancellation insurance policy for an additional $10 — just in case I would have been able to continue my odyssey in the opposite direction.

When consolidators are working within a prolonged time period, perhaps more than a year of travel time, it is possible to issue vouchers instead of actual tickets. The vouchers can then be stretched to more than a year whereas airlines do not issue actual tickets more than one year in advance, and vouchers insure there will be no increase in fare because the ticket has been paid (air fares are guaranteed once a ticket is paid).

Air passes are the way to go if you're covering long distances within a large country like Australia or Indonesia, or planning several international flights in Europe, or island hopping within a country or archipelago like Fiji or the West Indies. Almost all major airlines now have some kind of EuroFlyer program that connects major European cities; most stipulate that you must make your transatlantic flight with the carrier from which you want to purchase a EuroFlyer pass. However, Air France teams with Air Canada for flights within Europe, and Air Inter teams with several major airlines for a Le France Pass that reaches into all corners of France and parts of Switzerland.

Passes usually have to be purchased before you enter a country (not so in Fiji), and usually they are a substantial saving, but sometimes the minimum/maximum requirements and time limits make them cumbersome to fit into an itinerary. If you want a one-way flight London to Paris (because you're going back via the Chunnel on the new Eurostar train), you can probably get a better price from a wholesaler than using an airline's published pass fare. Senior discounts vary with these passes; don't forget to ask. Ironically, many passes cater to young travelers rather than to mature fun-seekers.

Travel agents and guidebooks have the facts about air passes. They exist from Argentina to India, so don't plan a trip until you gather air pass information. You may find you can arrange an itinerary within the required twenty-one days instead of the twenty-two days you were luxuriously allowing yourself; then

Parisian grandeur,
Musée du Petit Palais

surprise yourself with a few hundred dollars surplus in your budget. You also most likely will have to book specific flights so you will need to plan your routing. Fixed stops secure your routing which will probably be unchangeable; changes in date or time are easier to arrange, sometimes for an additional charge — *if* you can get a seat on your desired flight. I've heard many tales of travelers waiting two days for a thirty-minute local flight. Experience says it's better to book and try to adhere to the arranged schedule. You will avoid wasted time and possibly a missed flight home.

The charter airline business has undergone many upheavals in the years since deregulation. However, charter flights still exist. Air space on charter airlines may be combined with accommodations and sold as package tours to travel agents who in turn sell to the public; or organizations such as Conquest or Canada 3000 buy wholesale from charter airlines and then sell individual space to the general public. These flights are non-scheduled services which means the customer does not have access to other flights if the original flight is delayed or cancelled. One must wait until another charter plane arrives to pick up the slack. Usually charter flights are to specific tourist destinations, but because the flights are unscheduled, they are unpredictable. You may have been able to negotiate a low fare to Cancun, but when the return flight was bumped up twelve hours and the airline couldn't notify you during your scuba diving expedition, you were shifted to inconvenient rerouting and odd hours on whatever charter planes had space available. This is a typical scenario of charter flights, but it can be avoided if you take the time to frequently check with the airline close to departure day and to leave a current contact number with the office. Always pay for charter travel with a credit card which will provide a refund if the company defaults. If a charter company insists you pay cash directly to them, check their credentials with the US Department of Transport Public Charter Department, 400 Seventh SW, Washington, DC, 20590, phone (202) 366 2395 or with the International Air Transport Association, 2000 Peel Street, Montreal, Quebec, H3A 2R4.

Overland travel can include anything from an air-conditioned eight-hour bus journey from Chiang Mai to Bangkok, Thailand to a four-hour high-speed train ride on the TGV from Avignon to Paris or a sixteen-week truck/camping affair from Kathmandu to London. I have taken the eight- (read as twelve) hour bus ride in Thailand (the bus broke down a few times), and one way was enough (I flew north and bussed south); I've also sped to Paris on the marvellous TGV; I'm not even tempted to ensconce myself in an open truck for sixteen weeks with twenty-one strangers rattling across India, the Middle East, Africa, and parts of Europe. Maybe thirty years ago, but not today. If planning on Thailand in the near future, consider flying to the north, taking short bus and/or river trips, then returning to Bangkok by air to connect with your flight out of Thailand. French fast trains are fabulous, and there are a lot of alternatives to continuous overland transit from Nepal to England.

Traveling Europe by train is the preferred mode for many seniors. Carry your baggage on your back while you negotiate the station platforms and the train aisles, then relax with a cup of tea and catch up on your journal as the countryside glides by. If you travel in a sleeping car at night, you can save a hotel bill while getting from A to B. Time is a factor if you're considering several countries and a rail pass. Eurail passes are for specific time periods, and you may not save on a pass if you don't cover enough miles within a long enough period of time. Rick Steeve's company Europe Through the Back Door publishes a *Guide to European Railpasses.* Call (206) 771-8303 for a free copy. There are many seniors discounts available locally in Europe, and they may be cheaper than a Eurail pass. Britrail Pass offers a seniors discount, plus there is a British Rail Senior Railcard that gives even better discounts on some routes. If your travel agent doesn't know the details, contact the nearest Britrail and Eurail pass offices. Purchase these passes before leaving home, so time spent with a *Thomas Cook European Time Table* (ask your agent for an expired copy from which you can plan a general itinerary) can be dollars saved.

Eurobus is a new bus transportation system that operates non-smoking coaches (with guides) between most major West and East European cities. It is less expensive than train travel, possibly more secure, and is valid for either a two- or three-month period. The only public pickup spot is the Frankfurt airport; then you're on your own to select your individual routing using the hotel/hostel pickup and drop-off addresses that are supplied by the company. Phone (800) 517-7778 for a free information package.

If train or bus is not your overland choice, the obvious option is a rental car. All the large companies are price-competitive, so you, or your travel agent, need to shop around by calling the toll-free numbers for the best deal. If your European jaunt is for three weeks or more, look at leasing a car. Ask a lot of questions, especially about maximum age limits. Don't forget the taxes, mileage charges, drop-off penalties, time limits, territory limitations (it is now possible to take a rental car from Germany into

Driving on the other side, New Zealand

Eastern Europe but it's not allowed on the Ninety Mile Beach on the northern tip of New Zealand), currency exchanges, cancellation penalties, and the collision damage waiver if it's paid by your credit card. Check with your credit card company to make sure it still pays collision/damage insurance. Some companies are changing their policies. Research carefully such things as taxes—some countries may be several hundred dollars cheaper than others. Make sure your driver's license hasn't expired; you could even have difficulty with a temporary or replacement issue that is not precisely an original. You probably won't need an International Driver's License (available from C.A.A. or A.A.A) except for Central and South America (I did not need one in Costa Rica), Japan, and possibly Indonesia where you most likely will not drive yourself because, as in India, it is the social custom that you be driven. You can arrange for inexpensive hired cars with drivers at tourist information centers and hotels; considering the traffic and road conditions, don't attempt to drive yourself in these countries.

Left-hand driving can be unnerving at first, so try to avoid picking up a rental car at a downtown London or Sydney hotel. And if you can avoid it, don't drive in any large city. Park on the outskirts and take a local bus or train to the city center. I've parked for free in Greve, Italy in the lot beside the bus depot. Downtown Florence is only thirty minutes from Greve by bus. If driving in Turkey, leave the car in Yalova, across the Sea of Marmara from Istanbul, before venturing by ferry into yet another bustling, beautiful city. Drivingwith the Turks or the Italians is manageable in the country, but not in any kind of traffic congestion.

There is much to be said about driving overseas. Consult guidebooks and do extensive research with your travel agent before you decide to take on the hassles and tensions of foreign traffic and international road signs flashing past at 160 kilometers per hour on the autobahn. Another warning for North American drivers: make sure you can interpret local parking signs, and always carry local change for meters and coupon vending machines.

Dreams of faraway places with exotic names can bear fruit with TravLtip Cruise & Freighter Travel. This association claims that "unspoiled places still do exist, and you can sail there first class on a freighter for under $100 a day." TravLtips has been doing freighter business for more than twenty-five years now, and the bulk of their business has been with retirees. If you're interested in "unregimented days at sea and visiting ports all over the world," call (800) 872-8584 to become a member and receive their bi-monthly newsletter as well as other perks if booking a passage or just seeking information. TravLtips also specializes in small and unusual cruise destinations.

And, of course, for the ultimate in transoceanic sailing there is always the Queen Elizabeth 2. Cunard labels the QE2 "Tomorrow's Superliner Today." Pick up a brochure at your travel agent for transatlantic as well as cruise schedules on this refurbished floating palace. If four days of luxury for about $40,000 is your dream crossing, the QE2 has it; if you just want to watch, there are inside-inside staterooms for as low as $1,700 (1995); each fare includes sailing one way and flying the other way.

Chapter Four

Security

On your person: money belts, jewelery, papers

The Three Essentials that should accompany every traveler on their person are money, passport, and tickets. Money belts or fanny packs come in different shapes and sizes; don't purchase one that is too small to hold all the essentials. A medium-size leather fanny pack will hold glasses, comb, suitcase keys, and a couple of Handiwipe packets along with your Three Es. If planning river rafting or canoeing or hiking during a monsoon season, consider a waterproof pack. Whatever you choose, look for a sturdy leather or vinyl-coated nylon shell that cannot be cut easily, and a secure clasp. When the pack is tightly secured around your waist with the pouch and clasp in front, it is almost theft-proof. A sturdy pack in the proper position makes it likely you would feel a thief trying to cut the pack or undo the clasp. Another alternative is to carry the Three Es inside your clothing, although I find it uncomfortable to carry a packet of tickets in a pouch on a string around my neck, and perspiring in hot climates can damage a passport that fits snugly against your waist or leg. If I am in a particularly vulnerable situation, I carry most of my cash plus traveler's checks in an inside money belt, leaving change for immediate needs in my outside pack.

Fanny packs need more than one compartment plus a concealing flap to cover the access. Never display pack contents in public; keep small change in an outside section for easy accessibility. Never keep any of the Three Es in your pockets, including the zippered inside breast pocket of a sport coat or jacket. Pickpockets are faster and more adept than you can begin to imagine; their diversions and then speedy pilferage are disheartening to say the least. Rome train stations are plagued by rail-thin adolescent girls wrapped in rags, babies nursing at their breasts, challenging tourists to avoid giving them money. Their pushing and pleading tactics defy one to ignore them — make sure you keep your hands on your pouch until you get past the crush. I never encountered anything in India comparable to the scene in Rome, although invasive fingers are everywhere.

My sister-in-law returned home with a fractured nose after a motorbike mugging in Nice, France when a young man on a bike snatched her shoulder bag and pulled her to the ground when the strap secured across her chest didn't give way. In Orange, France a friend had her purse snatched from her hands inside a parked car while she was searching for some papers. The element played upon in these instances was surprise; my sister-in-law had been told to carry her purse with the strap across her chest, but she hadn't guessed the moving motorbike was after her money when she politely got out of its way and allowed herself to be cornered at the end of a street; my friend never dreamed someone would open her car door and grab her purse out of her hands. If both of these travelers had been carrying fanny packs, these thefts — and the broken nose — would probably not have occurred.

It seems that tourism begets thievery. The skill and expertise that abounds in tourist areas is truly astounding. As I was leaving my hotel in San José, Costa Rica to walk down the street to a

Only in Venice ... the Grand Canal

restaurant, the concierge suggested that I remove my gold necklace so it wouldn't get pulled off my neck and I wouldn't risk being injured. The gold chain was the only piece of jewellery I had with me; since then I have learned to leave all jewellery at home except for a plain gold wedding band, but even it has disadvantages. Some say it keeps conniving, lecherous men at a distance, but I wished I wasn't wearing it in Nepal when a ten year old girl insisted my ring — and my sunglasses and hiking shoes — were all better than her gold earrings and sparkling school uniform (including sturdy shoes) which just "weren't nice." Many foreigners have visions of North Americans as the proverbial "rich tourist" so the best advice is "don't look like one." Leave jewellery at home (in a safety deposit box at the bank), and carry your papers and money on your person in a simple, sturdy fanny pack or whatever kind of money belt you choose — just keep the Three Es out of sight and away from prying eyes and sticky fingers.

Don't risk leaving tickets or your passport at the hotel while out and about (some hotels will keep your passport overnight when you register — this is a matter of law in several countries — and international ships will keep your passport until you disembark). Passport reproduction is big business in many parts of the world. Don't contribute to world-wide fraud. Remember that if someone steals your passport and your tickets, you will be stranded for several days while your local embassy assists you. Stolen tickets mean a mess-up at the airline office; a stolen passport means a mess-up with your home government. Both will take several days to unravel. Read "As You Go: Emergency care" (page 130) for how to handle a missing passport and missing tickets.

Photocopying tickets before you leave is recommended; photocopies of the signature page of your passport is a necessity. Leave a copy at home with someone available to fax it to you if necessary, and stow a copy in the bottom of your suitcase. If your suitcase disappears, only the passport copy goes with it; if your passport disappears, you can produce a copy for the local consulate. Another hint is to also bring along your expired passport which would greatly expedite getting a replacement. I personally think that the more papers and copies you carry, the more vulnerable you are if thievery occurs. Most robbers want money or goods they can trade for money. Tickets can be copied or kept in hopes of a cash rebate if unused before the expiry date; passports will be sold to a passport reproduction ring; credit cards can be used to buy goods plus illegal identification. Make a copy of your credit card numbers, plus the phone numbers to call if they are lost or stolen, and keep them with your photocopied passport. Keep your traveler's check's registration numbers and agreement form separate from the checks.

Some say it's possible to use a passport photocopy when cashing traveler's checks, but I have never experienced this. If you are in a country where the tourist authorities retain your passport for your entire visit (used to be some areas of Russia and the Far East, but tourist's red tape is changing), you have no choice but to use a copy. This information you need to know before you go — see guidebooks and ask your travel agent. If a hotel in Western Europe or Southeast Asia unexpectedly insists on keeping your passport for an unduly long time, question the hotel management. Letting them know you are concerned will sometimes speed up their "regulations."

Carrying your passport with you at all times means you will always have it when you need it, even when you don't expect the need to arise. You will be able to reconfirm your ticket if you happen to walk past an appropriate airline office in the heart of a busy city (they will probably ask to see your passport), or to cash an extra traveler's check when you spy the perfect souvenir to send home, or more importantly, when you discover you're low on cash, it's thirty minutes before the banks close for a bank holiday (surprise!), and your passport is an hour away at your hotel.

The bottom line is — always keep the Three Es on your person, even in a Turkish bath where your pouch can remain within eyesight on the ledge of your bathing cubicle, or better still, with your traveling partner while you take turns in the bath. If you're swimming at a beach, leave your pouch with someone you trust and not behind a quasi locked door of a hotel room. (Read my comments below on safety deposit boxes.)

When referring to money, I include all forms, whether it's local currency, traveler's checks, or plastic money, (i.e., credit cards). It all lives in my fanny pack. Plastic cards (you won't need many; see "Money Matters: Credit cards" page 111) are filed in a small see-through case, and they are never left unattended. For extra local currency I carry a soft leather flat wallet which also has a belt loop on it (or a cloth money belt) for carrying inside my waist whenever I think it necessary to do so. Traveler's checks come in their own tidy plastic case, and tickets carried in a compact envelope wrapped in water-proof plastic snuggle against the rear of my fanny pack.

Personal property: safety deposit boxes, suitcases, equipment

The world over, hotels offer room safes for traveler's valuables — and in many cases these deposit boxes are violated by sophisticated thieves who obtain keys to copy or have access to combinations which make the boxes anything but safe. Occasionally, pried or tampered locks are evident on safes in the closets of hotel rooms. I have heard many horror stories from tourists who have lost all their money plus other valuables that they thought were safely deposited.

Some places have addressed the situation and instituted new measures. Most hotels in Hawaii now guarantee a central safety deposit box at the main desk (you may find a "use at your own risk" notice on your room safe) which is more inconvenient than leaving money in your room safe, but if you can't arrange for someone to watch your fanny pack while you swim or go for a snorkel, you have no choice. In more isolated areas where there are no obvious safes, you may have to ask the hotel management — not a clerk or a porter — to guard your pouch for you. In really out-of-the-way places, management has little control with next to no security, so your pack of valuables becomes your sole responsibility. Don't forget that your only real valuables are your money, passport, and tickets. Jewellery should always be left at home.

Virtually all travel handbooks or articles about security suggest the use of hotel room safety deposit boxes. After the tales I've heard, I find it difficult to follow these suggestions. Common sense is the best defence against thievery (no jewellery and no wallets in hip or breast pockets); it's usually our own carelessness that precipitates a loss. When my husband and I slipped our camera bag with a special lens to the car floor before we climbed out of our waiting taxi in Nairobi, we had no idea a gang of young thieves was watching us. When we returned to the taxi from the camera repair shop ten minutes later, our driver was very upset because we had left an article without telling him (he would have locked it in the trunk), and the theft occurred while the kids distracted him by getting him to move the taxi out of the way of another vehicle, allowing them to open the door and sneak the camera bag out of the car. Our driver wouldn't have known anything was taken if another driver hadn't seen it hap-

The law of the wild, Ngorongoro Crater, Tanzania

pen from across the street. Alas, it was our thoughtlessness that caused the problem. Later, when we filed a stolen goods report at the Nairobi police station, we followed a couple in the line-up (it was a long one) who had lost several thousand dollars from a Nairobi five-star hotel room safe. The hotel disputed the amount, and this was causing havoc with the couple's insurance claim (this was their third time in the line-up). A major difficulty with small, private safes is proof of deposit, although some systems have a central filing scheme that allows you to list contents with the management. Nevertheless, I would not rely on a safety deposit box to keep valuables safe.

At night, try and secure the pouch containing your passport, traveler's checks and airline tickets out of sight, possibly fastened to the bedpost near your head. If you are in the tropics and want cool breezes to drift over your sleeping body, choose a room at least one story up so the windows can remain open. Even a six-foot-deep plunge pool on the brink of a ground-floor bedroom's open sliding door will not deter a nighttime thief in the Caribbean.

East Africa is one place where nothing is left unattended. Two safari co-adventurers lost their daypacks with camcorders, prescription sunglasses, and all their toiletries when our guide assured us our open truck would be safe because the driver was in attendance while we shopped and went sightseeing around Arusha, Tanzania. The driver didn't see little urchins drop out of the trees in the side street where he had parked, and the two packs were lifted from the truck. We were extra cautious with locking everything in the baggage bins after that — we didn't even keep our packs in our tents at night. Thieves in Nepal — and in Africa, too, I suppose — have learned how to cut open tents during the night and steal packs while tired trekkers sleep.

Security can become a bigger problem than it needs to be. Common sense tells you to attach secure locks to travel packs or suitcases. Your luggage is vulnerable especially when left behind while on a trek or detour for a mini-excursion. Make sure the left-behind bags are securely locked, and double-check about leaving anything valuable, including your expired passport if you've taken it along. Locks can almost always be violated by an enterprising brigand, but hopefully a stout piece of metal will act as a deterrent.

Always lock luggage before it disappears into a transit baggage compartment. Airlines are notorious for rough handling that pops catches and seams. If your bags are not overstuffed and are locked, they stand a reasonable chance of surviving in one piece. Of course, carry-ons prevent a lot of harsh treatment of your bags (and save time waiting at baggage carousels), but it means packing very lightly. When I went around the world, I began with the good intentions of staying within carry-on limitations, but I soon got lazy and resorted to checking my travel pack, especially as most of my flights were non-stop direct. My heart sank when I happened to notice my pack stacked on a cart being wheeled out of the baggage claim area of the Delhi, India airport just as I was entering after waiting in an interminable passport lineup. That was the closest I came to losing my luggage.

There are several points to consider regarding lost luggage:

1) Report the loss immediately. Be firm but calm and don't accept a junior porter's advice to "wait and see." Usually your bag has been misrouted and can be traced, but you

need to start the tracing procedure immediately if the misrouting has taken your bag to Bombay instead of Delhi and you are leaving Delhi for London in twenty-four hours. There's a good chance everything will catch up with you before the next day's departure, or hopefully eventually in London, but you will endure more than a few nervous hours of waiting. In my early days of travel, my unlocked luggage failed to appear on a flight from San Francisco to Vancouver. When it finally was delivered to my home two days later, it had obviously been opened and searched by someone, presumably a customs official, according to the airline. Needless to say, I now always lock my suitcase.

2) Hold on to your baggage claim stubs. The personnel do not need them after all the numbers have been transferred to the claim forms, and the stubs offer proof if you have to resort to legal proceedings or insurance claims.

3) Check with the airline, or train, or bus regarding their official procedures to provision you while you wait. You may receive a travel kit or vouchers or possibly a reimbursed hotel bill if you can present receipts and verify the fact that you were delayed because of misplaced luggage.

4) Carry all of your necessities in your carry-on. Losing your jeans and sweater is an inconvenience; losing your prescription glasses and drugs could be life-threatening. Don't take a chance!

Missing or damaged equipment is another story. Professional photographers do not let their paraphernalia out of their sight if they can help it. If large props or tripods have to be stowed, they are usually carried "special handling." Most amateur photographic equipment can be hand-carried onto any transporting vehicle. Careful selection of a camera bag that holds all your lenses, filters, and gadgets is essential. Don't travel with one piece in one bag and another piece somewhere else. Choose a wide, sturdy shoulder strap for carrying the camera in front of you and not over your shoulder or towards your back when you are in crowds. Also, keep your film together — a separate waist pack works well — and insist it not go through the x-ray equipment in *most* airports. One exception is London/Gatwick which has installed state-of-the-art non-damaging radiography that has been tested by Kodak and guaranteed to be destruction-proof. If you notice that another airport's camera system is a moving video rather than a still photograph of baggage, it may be new enough to be non-damaging, but check with a supervisor before you risk your camera or your film. Sometimes the local personnel will insist you put your camera bag and film on their conveyor belts (Athens is particularly difficult), but you need to persevere and demand individual inspection. Call the security guards if necessary. Authorities will hand inspect rather than risk damage, but line workers simply want to push you and your equipment through the gate.

Be sure you register all equipment with the local customs office before you leave home. They will record the serial numbers of your cameras, binoculars, Walkman, notebook computer, even your bicycle to verify you left the country with them in your possession. If the equipment is lost or stolen, you can produce serial numbers for the police, and you also will have no difficulty proving when you re-enter that the goods were purchased before you left.

In spite of the fact that we had the serial numbers of our stolen lens and the camera people in Nairobi thought they knew where it might surface, there was no trace of the stolen goods when we checked during the next few weeks. We were not able to replace the lens until we returned home, where the insurance claim was greatly simplified because we had the serial number plus a copy of the Nairobi police report.

International air carriers will transport your bicycle, pedals removed (tape them onto the carrier rack), handle bars turned to the side, and tires half deflated, via "special handling." Record the serial number along with make, color, and model of the bike on your insurance agent's business card and stash it in your fanny pack. Of course you will carry a good bicycle lock, but that is no guarantee you will finish your walking tour of The Hague and find your bike where you left it.

Individual, group, and adventure tours

From Machu Picchu by narrow-gauge railway to high-tech play in Legoland, Denmark ... felluca sailing down the Nile, snorkelling the Great Barrier Reef, trekking the Annapurna Circuit along the way ... do you go by yourself, with a small group, or book an adventure tour?

There is no doubt that in many adventure hotspots of the world, there is safety in numbers, especially as undiscovered wonders no longer exist. Westerners are everywhere, and the influence of our culture is obvious. From the isolated San Blas Islands off the coast of Panama to remote Jayapura, Irian Jaya, metal antennae literally sprout on the roofs of grass huts. Natives sit mesmerized while *Rambo* and "Melrose Place" flit across their television screens that are powered by imported car batteries. While local customs may dictate that tribal peoples live in respectful harmony, that is not the picture portrayed of our civilization, and travelers are forced to bear the burden of false impressions. The entrepreneurial marketing of local crafts by Cuna Indians on San Blas is remarkable for its American-like tenacity; Irian Jaya's recent ex-head hunters (as little as thirty years ago) have learned how to steal from white-skinned *orang asings* (foreigners) with startling Rambo-like agility.

As Pico Iyer so succinctly says in *Video Night in Kathmandu*: "Every culture casts conflicting images before the world ... but in the case of America ... the contradictions are even more pronounced: for not only is the country's political power enormous, but it is matched — and sometimes opposed — by its cultural influence." Canadians claim some reprieve because they are known more as international peace keepers than political aggressors. Nevertheless, in Kathmandu, "Little House on the Prairie" remains more popular — and more available — than "Road to Avonlea," and the chance remains for travelers from anywhere in North America to be greeted with a confrontation between alien values and desires, sparked simply by their presence. Mediation by a tour leader's expertise with local contacts is often preferable to trying to establish isolated independent relationships with confused locals.

Fielding Guidebooks has a new title called *The World's Most Dangerous Places* (Macmillan Canada), but the advice is to get frequent updates regarding safe travel. The US Department of State, Bureau of Consular Affairs, Washington, DC 20524, issues travel advisories; the Citizens Emergency Center maintains a phone hotline — (202) 646-5225 from anywhere in the world — for the latest on safety information. The Canadian Department of Foreign Affairs provides current conditions in specific countries — phone (800) 267-6788 twenty-four hours a day, seven days a week.

No matter how independently one travels, local guides are a necessity. You will have to hire them whether you are in totally strange territory without maps, transportation or an interpreter, or whether it's "the law" to pay someone to walk along an obvious trail on a day-long mountain hike. Sometimes it's possible to avoid these legal impostors; other times it becomes a feat of patience and perseverance to outwit and outdistance unwanted local "expertise" (you've already read it in the guidebooks) that can be very annoying.

Joining a small group — possibly before you leave home — for an exploratory holiday, leaves the annoyance of misinformed guides to your tour leader. Traveling on your own and arranging everything as you go not only puts you directly in contact with the locals, but most likely will leave you in the vulnerable position of negotiating guide fees, transportation, and accommodation in a foreign language. This, of course, adds to the adventure, and for some intrepid travelers is the only way to see the world. Being open to the unexpected is of paramount importance for these people; being in good physical condition is equally important.

Lunchtime audience on the trail, Nepal

Don't attempt the impossible for your level of capability. Attach yourself to the security and support of a group if you cannot stay alert after trying to sleep on a thin foam pad on frozen ground or if traveler's diarrhea plagues you again. Not contending with travel logistics allows more energy for caring for your person and seeing what you came to see.

Adventure tours, ecotravel, educational adventures for older adults (Elderhostel and Interhostel, see "Appendix D" for addresses) have similar agendas if they are a reputable company. They should clearly state what your physical demands will be, what equipment you will need, what their itinerary involves. You need to know modes of transportation, meals provided, whether or not the itinerary is fixed or dependent on variable circumstances, what kind of equipment is provided by the company. Most adventure tour operators agree that the lower the price, the cheaper the equipment; you get what you pay for. As James Corbett of Canadian Outback Adventure Company, Ltd. writes in *Cast Travel News* published by the Canadian Association of Senior Travelers: "An equipment breakdown in the wilderness is not an adventure: it's a breakdown. And not much fun for anybody."

Investigate insurance policies, both your own and the company's, before you sign any waivers. Request references from previous customers; ask lots of questions. Is the company aware that you are a senior; are joining requirements compatible with your needs, such as smoking or non-smoking fellow travelers? Try to find a group that is sensitive not only to the wilderness ecosystems you are intruding upon, but also to the indigenous peoples who live there. How does the company handle entry into unfamiliar territory and contact with natives? How does the group leader address security concerns, and what precautions are deemed the responsibility of group members?

Adventure tours are a great way to reach into those remote corners of the world you never thought you would see. A big advantage is that they provide equipment — you won't have to bring along a kayak or a helmet or your own skis if you choose the proper outfitter. Keep your passport, traveler's cheques and airline tickets (see "Security: On your person," page 57) safely with you and explore!

Guarantees and insurance

"Guaranteed to be your thrill of a lifetime!" "Join our tour for the ultimate journey of discovery." "Be adventurous — be brave! Pay now to reserve your place on our exciting expeditions."

Wait. Before you sign on the dotted line, read all about it. "Essential facts" need to be just that; if they are couched in unclear terminology, check them out. What does the term "salubrious hotel" mean? Will you feel shortchanged if you've paid what you thought was fair price for a comfortable hotel reprieve after two weeks roughing it in the bush, only to be greeted by a dirty room and cold shower? Being warned that this may be the only accommodation available when you move out of your tent tells you what to expect, plus gives an idea of what the approximate cost should be. But if you've been lured by and paid for the promise of a hot shower and clean sheets, chasing cockroaches will not make you a satisfied customer.

Reputable tour companies know this, and they try to maintain their reputation so they can stay in business. When they clearly state their objectives along with an outline of their commitment plus your responsibility to meet those objectives, don't ignore the line that says "if this is not acceptable to you, do not come with us." No matter how much you want to see Antarctica, if your hope is for calm seas for the advertised thirty-two hour boat crossing over some of the roughest seas in the world, you are not going to have a good time with this expedition. Choose a kayaking adventure in Greenland instead.

Of course you can go on your own — without a company to share the risks and the responsibility — but you will still have to hire a guide, outfit yourself, and spend probably twice as much money getting there and getting around, as well as buying your own insurance. Current standard liability coverage for adventure tour companies is $1,000,000 — some go as high as $5,000,000. As a member of a tour group you will probably be asked to sign a waiver which forgoes your right to make certain claims on the company. If your hotel accommodation has turned out to be less than expected, all you can do is write letters of complaint; if you suffer a personal injury due to faulty equipment or an act of carelessness on the part of the company, you can claim compensation if you haven't waived your right to do so. Some waivers are acceptable because you have purchased your own travel health and accident insurance. But there are always clauses for situations not covered, and this is where insurance confusion begins.

Travel health and accident insurance is a world of its own. It's not difficult to sort out, but it does require some detective work.

If you are away from your home country frequently, consider buying a commuter's annual policy in place of individual coverage for each trip; your total premium may be lower for the entire year than several short-term policies. Single-trip policies can be purchased for up to six months (183 days) of continuous travel. This coverage is in addition to your at-home policy which you will continue to pay while you are traveling. If you are going around the world for more than six months, you have homework to do. Extension clauses exist — you just have to find them.

The best person to assist with the myriad travel medical policies is often your family insurance broker. Ask for the best quotes the agency can find; do your own leg work with automobile club travel insurance, employee insurance plans, credit card policies, or whatever else you may stumble across — then compare. You will have to read all the conditions, benefits, restrictions, start and stop times, claim instructions, repatriation rules, travel partner coverage, etc. This requires time. Don't wait until the last minute to purchase extended medical insurance. Travel agents also sell insurance. In fact some travel insurance companies deal exclusively with travel agents. When you seek travel insurance information from both your travel and insurance agencies, you will learn the ins and outs.

Many insurance companies offer travel packages. An example for Canadians is Voyageur Insurance based in Brampton, Ontario. Voyageur's travel package, described in brochures distributed to travel agents, includes cancellation and interruption, emergency medical, baggage and personal effects, flight accident and travel accident insurance all in one premium. Medical care is provided world-wide through the company's group of doctors and hospitals under the umbrella of Assured Assistance, Inc. Contact instructions and multilingual interpreter services are included, all of which can be a distinct advantage in developing countries. The amount of medical coverage paid is unlimited, but there are age and travel-time limitations, the usual pre-existing condition clauses, and possibly duplication if your personal effects are covered by your homeowner's policy, and flight and travel accidents are sometimes covered by the emergency medical policy on your credit card.

An American company, TravMed, offers Americans $100,000 medical protection for $3.50 per day through age 70, and $5 per day age 71 to 80. Travel Guard International sells coverage through US travel agencies. You may purchase their extended medical protection for reimbursement to you for your direct payments; it has no deductible, no daily limits, and emergency evacuation.

Best oranges in the world, Cyprus

Their underwriter is Transamerican Occidental Life, 1145 Clark Street, Stevens Point, WI 54481, phone (800) 782-5151. Another American company is Access America, 600 Third Avenue, Box 807, New York, New York 10163, phone (800) 284-8300.

When my husband and I traveled from Canada (excluding the USA) for eight months, we purchased a $1,000,000 Excess Hospital/Medical policy through our insurance agent. The insurance is administered by Travel Underwriters of 302-5811 Cooney Road, Richmond, BC, Canada V6X 3M1 and underwritten by Canadian Group Underwriters Insurance Company. We paid $1 per day for myself, age 55, and $2 per day for my husband, age 66. We were able to extend the policy for the last two months (by fax from Israel) after assuring the company that we were still in good health and had made no claims during the previous six months. Our provincial insurance continued coverage because we assured the home office before we left that we were traveling and had full intention of returning to reside in the province. (The usual provincial cut-off for out-of-province coverage is six months.)

Reading the small print and understanding pre-existing condition clauses cannot be overemphasized, especially for mature travelers. Most policies state that health problems arising or chronic conditions undergoing change in treatment within sixty days of the effective starting date of the policy will not be covered; some revert back as long as six months. If you have a stable cardiac condition that has not required medical attention during those six months, and then experience enough angina at the Moulin Rouge to warrant a checkup at a Paris hospital, the company will probably pay. If, on the other hand, your medication was changed six weeks before you left home, you will be paying the electrocardiogram costs yourself. Effective starting date is a key point; it can mean the day you apply for the policy rather than the day you begin your trip (which is when you start to pay). Double-check the fine print if you have any kind of chronic health condition that may be affected by the stress of travel.

Beware of insurance duplication. You may decide not to have any additional medical coverage if you're traveling to New Zealand where their accident-compensation scheme covers everyone, irrespective of fault or country of residence, and the risk of contacting a disease is very low (no malaria, for instance). However, the accident insurance stops at repatriation, so once you leave New Zealand you're on your own, dead or alive.

Trip cancellation/interruption insurance is important. Airline and ground transportation tickets purchased in advance at low rates are usually nonrefundable; everything from moderately priced adventure tours to expensive cruises will refund only a certain percent within a specified time before departure date. If you have to cancel because of illness three days before you're scheduled to leave, or you have to interrupt the trip to return home because of a death in the family, you stand the chance of a substantial financial loss if you haven't bought adequate cancellation insurance. Buying from the same company that runs the tour is acceptable providing the company is well established. In fact, some companies insist you buy from them or sign a waiver stating that you have declined their insurance. If you have purchased a travel insurance package with a cancellation policy that

Routeburn Trail hikers, South Island, New Zealand

covers the full cost of the tour, you don't have to duplicate your policy with the tour company, and signing the waiver is okay. But be sure your policy has adequate coverage. Often it's just barely enough for a return economy airfare. The usual cost of tour cancellation insurance is 5 percent of the total price, so coverage for a $5,000 tour will be about $250. Tour companies that cover themselves with their own "insurance" often mean that once you've paid your money, you won't get a refund if you have to cancel, but you will be able to reschedule at a later date.

Another safety measure to consider before leaving is to increase your credit card limit as an emergency measure. You may need extra cash to pay up front and be reimbursed later. Knowing there is an extra few thousand available if you need it is reassuring to yourself as well as a foreign hospital admitting office.

Many adventure travel companies require that you purchase evacuation insurance. You will find it in the fine print of extended medical benefits. If it's not there, change the policy for one that carries it. Policies are quite definitive regarding conditions covered or excluded. I doubt that very many mature adventurers will be concerned if they aren't allowed to bungee-jump, but flying glider planes may be on the agenda. Make sure your insurance covers your soaring, plus evacuation if you're bound for a wilderness expedition.

Extra baggage insurance is usually superfluous because personal property is covered by homeowner's policies. Airlines have minimal coverage because they know you are covered already; their maximum is approximately $635 per piece of checked baggage on international flights. You may need to insure a specific item for an appraised amount (have the serial numbers handy) before you leave if your homeowner's policy states it will pay only depreciated values.

The best insurance against bankruptcy and nondelivery of promised services comes with your credit card. Credit card companies provide comprehensive protection when you use their piece of plastic to pay for travel. When you purchase transportation on a common carrier with your credit card, you are almost always covered for travel accident insurance (although sometimes for a low sum). Most major cards still cover rental car collision damage waivers (CDW), but some are dropping this coverage, so check the latest information on your card before you sign a rental car contract. See "Money Matters: Credit cards," page 111, for more on credit card usage.

A hint from a travel agent who specializes in around the world ticketing: instead of trying to reroute in the event of an emergency, move your schedule up. If the next leg on your consolidated ticket is Delhi to London, with perhaps a side trip in Europe, and then home across the Atlantic, your best chance of getting home fastest is to continue with your Delhi-London flight and on to North America immediately. Exchanging times instead of routes is less complicated and time consuming because you will be working with a foreign airline that issued tickets to a wholesaler months before, and their system of payment is difficult to adjust. The airline may even force the tickets back to the issuing agency to change routing. If you can possibly continue in your planned direction, do so. You will get home faster, using tickets that you already have purchased. In most cases you will eventually receive a refund for the unused side trip to Europe.

I was lucky when Egypt's tourism industry collapsed in 1994 due to terrorist scares, after I had purchased my ticket to Cairo and during my travels in Africa. When I decided to change flights from Kenya Airlines, Nairobi to Cairo, to Elal Airlines, Nairobi to Tel Aviv, I had no difficulty in getting Air India who had originally issued the ticket for Kenya Air to endorse the change to Elal (for an additional fee). If there hadn't been an Air India office in Nairobi, I'm not sure what would have happened, but Kenya Air was aware of the political situation, which international airline codes recognize as good reason for cancellation and refund. Luckily, I did not have to purchase a replacement ticket and wait for a refund.

Insurance checklist:

1) Travel medical

Q. Is the coverage enough?

check: limitations, conditions, deductible

Q. Which care providers are covered?

check: those exclusively under the umbrella of an insurance company, reimbursement of a percentage of expenses you have incurred over and above your private or government insurance plan, coverage of: anaesthetist, physiotherapist, lab tests and x-ray, ambulance, emergency out-patient care, prescription drugs

Q. What are the pre-existing condition exclusions?

check: time restrictions, age limitations, controlled condition definition, pre-existing condition definition, effective date of policy

Q. Is there an out-of-pocket allowance during hospitalization of a traveling companion?

check: family transportation expense coverage

Q. How is medical care paid?

check: pay up front and reimbursed, file a claim, how to file a claim

Q. How do you arrange for health care?

check: contact numbers, multilingual services, toll-free help line

Q. Is emergency medical evacuation covered?

check: limits of coverage, under what conditions, return of vehicle

Q. Is repatriation covered?

check: repatriation of deceased, cremation, return of vehicle coverage

Q. How do you extend the policy?

check: extension fee charged, who to contact

Q. What activities, and possibly what countries, are not covered?

check: mountaineering, water sports, Algeria, Afghanistan, Bosnia

2) Trip cancellation/interruption

Q. What are the covered risks?

check: natural disasters, accident on way to departure, terrorist activity

Q. What benefits are paid before AND after departure?

check: maximum limit, coverage of traveling companion

Q. How do you file a claim?

check: requirements for unused tickets to insurer, physician attendance rules

Q. What constitutes validity of policy?

check: when to purchase, effective dates

3) Personal effects/baggage coverage

Q. What is covered under homeowner's policy?

check: amount of coverage of personal effects in transit, depreciated versus appraised value for replacement, exclusions of policy (currency, furs, jewellery, art), additional floater or rider required for special equipment

Q. Is baggage insurance in a travel package redundant?

check: individual amounts of necessary policies versus package premiums, will insurer collect payment from your homeowner's policy before settling your claim

4) Collision damage protection

Q. Does your credit card cover CDW only if you pay with their card?

check: insurance available through a travel underwriter if not using a credit card and vice versa

Q. Does car rental company recognize credit card coverage?

check: specific card collision coverage in specific countries (for example, MasterCard while driving from Western to Eastern Europe)

check: countries or states that disallow CDW (for example, Hawaii)

5) Travel accident insurance

Q. Is this redundant in view of excess medical insurance?

check: age limitations, exclusions

Chapter Five

Before Leaving Home

At-home details: mail, house, car, pets

Our homes require tender loving care whether we are in residence or not. Condominiums nestled behind security gates and festooned with silk plants almost take care of themselves while owners are away. However, changing lights and window coverings to give a lived-in look is better than a static appearance. A house and garden obviously demand more attention than a condo, but the same rule applies. A housesitter will need to be hired to look after the home and collect mail while you are away. This is an unavoidable expense of travel, as is arranging for pet care. Ideally, the person who is looking after the house can also look after the animals rather than placing the pets in a boarding kennel. Professional housesitters are listed under House Sitting or Sitter Services in the *Yellow Pages*; check with the Better Business

Bureau and local police for complaints; ask for references.

Friends looking for a change of scenery have stayed in our island home, I have hired strangers to housesit, plus rented for long-term absences which, of course, produced revenue instead of depleting my bank account. All of these arrangements have been more than satisfactory except one, when I returned home to a mess in the house and yard plus some minor damages. A housesitter, referred by a friend, simply didn't understand what her responsibilities included. An informal written agreement would have helped, especially with regard to paying a salary. The situation was an unfortunate consequence of my wanderlust, but it wasn't a major disaster. And I'm convinced there is a higher risk in leaving one's home unoccupied.

Homeowner insurance policies vary, but usually there is a clause excluding fire and theft coverage of vacant premises with time limits and restrictions clearly stated. Check the policy, and also check if a housesitting agency is bonded and insured to cover theft and damages. Bonded companies are adequate for the length of absence your policy will cover, usually fifteen to thirty days. If you are on an extended trip and your neighbor becomes your long-term housesitter from a distance, you may face the task of convincing your insurance underwriter that someone was close enough to discover that smouldering electrical fire before it caused a huge amount of damage. If you decide to have a renter or to sublet, remember to change the utilities to the new occupant's name, plus pass their identity on to your insurance agent. The best of all possible worlds could be a house exchange, but this doesn't work if you are vagabonding and not confined to one location. See "Appendix C" for home exchange organizations.

However you leave your home, you need to leave instructions. The basement light only goes on if the stairwell remains lit, the garburator runs when the sink plug is inverted, the VCR is probably unplugged, use only liquid cleaner on the marble sinks in the bathroom. Prepare a Home Care Book and keep it up to date. The more you travel the more thrilled you will be when you can fall back on your instruction book; it's very reassuring to know your home has its own backup system for care. Be sure to list which neighbor or business to call for what kind of emergency.

If you are leaving your car for someone else to use, make sure the insurance and registration will continue until you return. Vehicles can be secured in storage facilities if no one will be driving them for several months. Check with your mechanic for any storage care precautions that should be taken.

Business details: banks, accountants, lawyers, taxes

Not only do you need a reliable housesitter, but you need someone to look after your business affairs as well. Traveling for a month or even six weeks is no problem; you can deal with mail and bills when you get home. All that is needed is someone to collect your mail while they look after your home.

If the trip is longer than six weeks it becomes more complicated. You will need someone to open your mail, pay bills, make bank deposits, possibly keep you financially solvent as you go. When I have traveled more than two months, I have hired a local accountant who obtains signing privileges at my bank, and to whom I've entrusted my mail key (if your house is rented, you may be able to temporarily redirect your mail to another address) along with my bank safety deposit box key attached to my lawyer's business card. This person is then responsible for collecting my mail, paying bills, depositing money at the bank, and notifying my lawyer in case of emergency. I check in as often as is convenient by telephone, which sometimes isn't necessary at all. It's surprising how business affairs take care of themselves when you're away, providing you have taken the time to make proper arrangements before you go.

Before I leave, my bank manager agrees to make credit card payments directly from my account, I redirect the credit card statements to the bank, and I establish a line of credit with the bank to cover overdrafts and emergencies. I also increase my credit card limits as another emergency measure. I discuss my travel plans with the bank officials who are willing to check my account regularly to ensure I am not overdrawn. If money needs to be transferred from my line of credit, the manager will do so.

The drawback to having someone other than yourself make your credit card payments is that you cannot check the statements until you return from your trip. If you are really concerned (especially if your limit is sky high), you could keep your own running account of charges incurred, then fax or telephone the figures every month to your bill-paying accountant who in turn can be the payee instead of the bank. (Having your own idea of what the running total should be is especially helpful if a card is lost or stolen.) Some credit card companies and banks now have direct payment plans from your account; your manager or other bill-payer doesn't have to be involved—but you still cannot check statements until you get home. This makes one doubly vigilant while traveling to watch when a credit card is imprinted. For more on credit cards see the sections "Security: On your person" (page 57) and "Money Matters: Credit cards" (page 111).

When I return home from a lengthy trip, for a nominal monthly fee to my local accountant my affairs are in order, with current bookkeeping to show banking done, money deposited, bills paid; and the mail, including last season's Christmas cards, is neatly piled in a box.

All income tax material, including annual retirement savings plan payments, was left in the hands of my tax accountant (along with a few blank checks) who compiled the basics of my annual return before I left. (He knew I would be home in time to catch up on payments.) Canadians are unable to obtain extensions for filing annual returns; Americans can apply for an extension if they are going to be out of the country. Consult with your local tax expert for details before you leave.

Decisions about investment strategies are left to my financial advisor; power-of-attorney has been left with my lawyer along with a copy of my itinerary plus next of kin addresses and instructions regarding the whereabouts of my updated will.

Yes, it's a lot of work. And planning. But you don't want to be thinking about income tax in March or April while you are on safari in Africa (faxes are hellishly expensive both sending and

Solo lioness, Serengeti National Park, Tanzania

receiving in Tanzania). In fact, it's so much work to prepare for extended travel, you may as well stretch your adventures as long and as far as possible. If your line of credit at the bank will cover you for a year — go for it! And if your age is creeping up to the limits for reasonable rates for extended medical coverage, don't wait!

Other preparation points to remember include property taxes that will come due and insurance renewals — medical, car, house and personal property. If you don't already have one, a safety deposit box at the bank is essential for important papers and a copy of your will, plus valuable jewellery. Other valuables in your home such as silver, art, and antiques can be insured or stored in a safe. Your best form of house protection and peace of mind is a high quality installed alarm system that is connected to a local security office (who you have notified about your housesitter).

Travel details: tourist visas, immunizations

Sandwiched between business and house details come more travel details. Your itinerary has been sketched out and flight reservations are pending. Dates and destinations are secure enough for you to now pursue visa application and immunization schedules. Medical advisors say to allow at least three months prior to departure to update an International Certificate of Vaccination. You will need six months for a full tetanus/diphtheria series if you are not eligible for a booster, and five months for Hepatitis B vaccine if you will be working in health care fields or living in a high risk area more than six months. Ask your doctor about Havrix, the new Hepatitis A vaccine. Tourist visas are usually valid for entry three months from issuing date (some may stretch for six months or possibly a year).

Visa requirements are always subject to change. Don't rely on what your neighbour told you about visiting France six years ago (there was a temporary ruling for US and Canadian passport holders to obtain a visa), or on what someone with a Canadian passport says about entry into Kenya (in 1994 Canadians didn't need a visa; Americans did). You must either consult the relevant embassy or consulate of the country you wish to visit, or ask your travel agent for current details. Travel agencies are served by visa procuring businesses that supply application forms and a list of requirements (how many photos, interview or by mail, how long visa is valid for) and how much the fees are. Given enough time, along with your passport and completed application forms, the visa service will obtain your tourist visas for you (providing a personal interview is not involved). But there's a hitch....

When I went to Kenya (I have a US passport), I had to obtain my visa in Delhi because I left home more than three months before my arrival in Nairobi. The total cost to me at the Kenya Consulate in Delhi was Cdn$14.50 for a double entry visa. The fee via the visa service through my travel agent was quoted at Cdn$73.50 if I allowed two weeks processing time, more if I needed my passport returned in a hurry. After writing to the Kenya High Commission in Ottawa where I discovered that I could not purchase a visa more than three months before my entry date, I also discovered that had I been within the required time frame, the Ottawa consulate would have charged me Cdn$20

Riding the carpets, Kathmandu, Nepal

(Cdn$10 for single entry), and processed my application within a week. Every embassy sets their own fees (Ottawa's charges do not dictate Delhi's price), and service charges are set by independent companies. Traveler beware!

There are all kinds of wrinkles in obtaining visas. A few months before I arrived in Nepal in 1994, their visa fee doubled (from $20 to $40, payable in US currency only), which meant standing in line at the exchange window because I didn't have enough US change, and then standing in the visa line; the whole process taking more than an hour. India charged twice as much for same-day service as it would have cost if I had been able to leave my passport at the consulate overnight. A Malaysian travel agent processing Thai visas charged more for overnight service because I would not hand over my onward airline tickets plus my passport to accompany my application for entry into Thailand. When the agent refused to accept a photocopy of my tickets but offered to let me keep my tickets if I paid an additional fee, I decided to pay the extra $30 rather than surrender my total traveling security blanket for twenty-four hours. Who can know what surprise is waiting in the next visa office or consulate? Two things seem to be standard: increased fees for faster service, and confiscation of your passport — no copies — while your visa is being processed, usually at least twenty-four hours.

When applying to several different countries before you go, make allowances for the time it takes to process a visa application. Each consulate will need your passport for however long their processing and mailing takes — sometimes as long as two weeks. Start visa applications as soon as you know you are within the required travel time frame. You may have an option on either regular or registered mail return, or you may be required to pay the insured mailing costs whether or not speed of return is a factor.

If you are traveling around the world, check on individual countries' visa requirements before you leave and take the specified number of passport size photos with you — some countries require two, some only one. This will save you a lot of hassle while traveling. Visa photos do not have to be officially stamped passport photos, just recent and of passport size. My husband and I did a photo session (using a tripod) in our living room, had several copies made, then cropped them ourselves. Also, photocopy your onward travel tickets for the countries for which you will be applying en route. Some officials will accept a photocopy of your official (from the travel agent) itinerary in lieu of copied tickets, especially if you're purchasing a ferry or train or bus ticket as you leave the country.

Israeli security is especially tight, so have as many official papers as possible readily available when going through any Israeli port of entry checkpoint. In April, 1994 I paid a fee for a visa stamp upon entry into Israel which, like Nepal, was paid in US dollars. In light of the discrepancies between rates published in guidebooks and actual prices, keep US dollars in reserve for visa emergencies; the amount will depend on how many visas you anticipate having to obtain. Australia requires a tourist visa good for three months on each entry to Australia within the year for which the visa is issued, and there is no charge for the visa (current information October, 1995). Write, telephone or fax the embassies of the countries you are visiting if you want accurate and up-to-date information. Embassies are listed in major city phone directories under Consulate General and the specific country.

Make sure your passport is not going to expire while you are traveling. Many countries require that your passport remain valid for six months from the issuing date of your visa before they will allow you across their border. Apply for an early renewal if necessary.

As if visas aren't enough to think about, your health records need attention, too. Regardless of your life style and medical preferences, immunizations for international travel are a necessity. You cannot go without them. The only exemptions are because of age (infants under six months or children under two years), and on medical grounds if a physician signs and dates a statement on the physician's letterhead giving reasons vaccination should not be performed. To quote the Centers for Disease Control and Prevention *Health Information for International Travel*, US Department of Health and Human Services: "There are no other acceptable reasons for exemption from vaccination."

If you are a serious and frequent international traveler, you need a copy of CDC's latest *Health Information for International Travel.* The book is reissued every year and presents a thorough overview of vaccination requirements as well as health hints for travelers. Biweekly updates called Blue Sheets give such information as the latest reports of cholera and yellow fever. The book is for sale in the US from the Superintendent of Documents, US Government Printing Office, Washington, D.C., 20402, and through Renouf Publishing Company, 1294 Algoma Road, Ottawa, ON, K1B 3W8 in Canada. Blue Sheets are available upon request.

CDC has an automated traveler's hotline in the US available twenty-four hours a day, seven days a week, from a touch-tone phone (404) 332-4559, or fax (404) 332-4565. The fax line will supply copies of the Blue Sheet as well as other disease risk and outbreak bulletins. Canadians may phone the International Association for Medical Assistance (IAMAT) at (519) 836-0102, 40 Regal Road, Guelph, Ontario N1K 1B5. Both organizations work

Klotok at Jungle Lodge, Kalimantan, Indonesia

with the World Health Organization, and it is WHO that establishes international health regulations. Vaccinations such as typhoid or an injection of serum immuno-globulin may be administered by your family physician or a public health nurse; yellow fever vaccinations are given only in designated official centers which are responsible for validating your international certificate at the time of vaccination with a signature and an official "Uniform Stamp."

This may sound like a lot of unnecessary rules and regulations, but WHO takes your health seriously, hoping you will do so also. As soon as you have your itinerary organized, contact your public health department or travel clinic to which your family doctor refers you. You will need a record of your previous immunizations. Knowledgeable personnel will check the current requirements for the countries you are visiting, and give you a schedule for vaccinations and any other prophylactic measures they deem necessary, especially protection against malaria. Whatever you do, do not take malaria lightly. It is very prevalent in many areas, and strains are becoming more and more resistant to the antimalarials in common use. Contrary to popular belief, the disease still kills many, many people every year. You need the advice of your physician along with a prescription for which malaria medications to take, when.

Before you leave checklist:

1) At home details

   Q. Where do I start?

   check: vacancy clause of homeowner's insurance policy, housesitter, housesitting business' insurance/bonding, outside care, inside care, pet care, newspaper cancellation, mail collection, Home Care Book

   Q. What if I rent or sublet my home?

   check: homeowner's insurance requirements, utility changes, damage deposit, property manager

   Q. What can I do with my car?

   check: storage requirements, insurance if someone else using

2) Business details

   Q. Where do I start?

   check: length of trip: six weeks or less, mail and business accumulation; more than six weeks, business manager, mail key or address change, bank safety deposit box key with lawyer's business card, bank signing privileges, checkbook, written instructions for paying bills and handling correspondence and banking

   check: bank manager and credit card payments, line of credit, transfer of moneys, discussion of travel plans

Q. What do I HAVE to remember?

check: annual income tax return, annual retirement savings plan payments, investment strategies, power-of-attorney, update of will

Q. What else do I need to remember?

check: property taxes, medical and car and home-owner's insurance payments, jewelery and will in bank safety deposit box, increase credit card limits

3) Travel details

Q. How do I arrange tourist visas?

check: travel agent or guidebook for country requirements, consulate for current length of validity time and fees and application forms, how many photos, visa service through travel agent, how long to process

Q. How do I obtain visas en route?

check: foreign consulate addresses in which cities, how many photos, photocopy of outgoing tickets or itinerary, time frame for obtaining visa

Q. What about my passport?

check: expiry date, early renewal if less than six months to expiry

Q. What health records do I need?

check: International Certificate of Vaccination update, call hotline or check with travel clinic for current requirements

Q. How much time do I need for immunizations?

check: which immunizations for where, coordination of series of inoculations, advance antimalarial medications

Chapter Six

The Healthy Traveler

Preventive medicine

For a discussion on immunization schedules see "Travel details" (page 84). Antimalarial medications need to be discussed with a family physician who may in turn refer you to a travel clinic where experts will answer questions as well as determine the best program for you to follow. They will need to know your drug allergies, current medications, specific areas of travel, and how you will be traveling (air-conditioned hotels versus tenting). They will prescribe medication and give general advice as well as instruction on personal protection. Most medication regimes begin two weeks before you travel. As stated previously, do not take malaria lightly.

For further reading about health issues I highly recommend the Centers for Disease Control book *Health Information for International Travel*, and *Don't Drink the Water* co-published by the Canadian Public Health Association and the Canadian Society for International Travel (see "Appendix B" for mail order information). *Don't Drink the Water* is more detailed concerning high altitude sickness; *Health Information for International Travel* is more specific regarding which countries require vaccinations and malaria protection. Both are worth reading if you are a long-term traveler to high risk areas, or an adventure traveler versus someone who confines themselves to resort areas. Updates are available from the CDC hotline at (404) 332-4559 from a touch-tone phone, or the International Association for Medical Assistance (IAMAT) at (519) 836-0102 in Canada. Another book worth knowing about is *The Pocket Doctor* by Stephen Bezruchka, M.D. published by The Mountaineers, ISBN 0-89886-345-7. You can actually carry this tiny edition in your travel kit bag, but I suggest a pre-trip visit to a pharmacist for interpretation of the generic drug names used in the medicine tables plus some supplementary suggestions for diarrhea and motion sickness.

Mature travelers cannot be too careful when it comes to protection against foreign organisms that wreak havoc with healthy bodies. Traveler's diarrhea is something that plagues everyone in a foreign environment sooner or later. A home remedy that works particularly well is the use of yogurt capsules or lactobacillus acidophilus. Buy yogurt capsules from a health food store, and take one every day two weeks before travel to developing countries or any place with a diet totally different from your usual, then one capsule a day during the actual trip. When, or if, diarrhea does attack, I take a Kaopectate® tablet along with the yogurt capsule, and I'm usually cured. Prolonged or severe diarrhea requires a doctor's attention.

Follow the rules about drinking only purified water and eating only fresh foods that you can clean or peel yourself (everything else must be well cooked or boiled) and you stand a chance of staying healthy.

A major consideration for every healthy traveler is water purification. I was amazed to find sealed bottled water for sale in remote villages of Nepal, but I soon learned that wherever trekkers go, locals capitalize on potential customers. Because I could buy water, I didn't use my purifier, but it is a handy gadget to have. Make sure you buy a purifier and not just a filter. The PUR Scout is a microbiological water purifier that contains a microfilter that removes micro-organisms larger than one micron (like giardia cysts) plus a tri-iodine resin that kills smaller bacteria and viruses. The cartridges are expensive to replace, and the cylinder is rather bulky to carry, but it costs less to use than buying bottled water, which is twice the price of beer in Tanzania. All water can be simply treated with iodine tablets, but the best treatment is a full rapid ten-minute boil. Electric immersion heaters for individual cups may be effective for one cup at a time, but if the water supply is grossly questionable, treat the water with iodine tablets first. Travelers with thyroid conditions need to discuss the use of iodine with their physician before relying on iodine purification. An alternative is more expensive ceramic water purifiers which have very fine micron filters and do not use iodine.

Health risks for travelers are not confined to food and water. Jet lag can be debilitating; your biological clock gets desynchronized, you don't sleep or eat properly, and your autoimmune system takes a beating. The recirculated air in an aircraft exposes you to cold and flu germs, and bingo — you're sick. Being run-down or overtired from last minute rushing before a trip also allows unwanted organisms to settle on you — you don't have to wait for jet lag. Try to board an initial long flight well rested. Use the check lists in this book to help with planning and organization, allow *lots* of time, and remember that most travelers agree that it's easier to acclimatize when traveling in a westward direction. A common suggestion for combating jet lag is to allow one day of adjustment for each time zone you cross. From the west coast of North America to London, England is eight zones, so your body will take about a week to become totally acclimatized if you travel eastwards. Drink lots of non-diuretic liquids while traveling, and think about resorting to a mild sleep sedative if your body clock doesn't reset within a reasonable length of time. There are numerous other remedies for jet lag that alter your pre-trip sleep

Crooked windows and shrinking posts, The Shambles, York, England

and diet patterns as well as exposure to light. Check your library or travel bookstore for the latest information on overcoming jet lag.

The use of eye shields is a health measure because they help you sleep. Keep a pair handy in your carry-on or day pack. Make sure your belongings are secure before blackout, then arrive refreshed because you have slept through the dated Woody Allen movie on a plane or the kung fu masterpiece on a bus video. Another aid to peaceful rest and rehabilitation is a Walkman with earphones which can block out noise while providing musical peace and tranquility.

Insect repellent is a necessity. In a malarial area, you need something strong, preferably containing DEET. Citronella and Avon's *Skin-So-Soft* are less effective alternatives. Anopheles mosquitoes bite between dusk and dawn, their peak times being from midnight to four in the morning. No matter when they bite, you can't feel it because of the local anaesthetic they so kindly inject along with their blood parasite. Stay indoors at night, under a mosquito netting when you sleep, and use a mosquito coil in your room. Almost all hotels and guest houses in mosquito infested areas supply coils; some have mosquito nets. Carry matches or a small butane cigarette lighter for lighting coils. Another hint is to wear cover-up clothes like long sleeve shirts and long pants after the sun sets. If you are really worried about insect bites, tote your own bed net, put it in place early, and tuck it around the mattress. You may find that it is too warm because it impedes circulation, and you will not want to use it. Check the CDC hotline or with IAMAT (see "Appendix B" for phone numbers) for areas of increased reporting of malaria, especially the chloroquin-resistant strains. Dar es Salaam and Zanzibar on the east coast of Africa were particularly virulent in 1994. If the advisory for the area for which you are headed is to carry mosquito netting, try to find one with mesh that isn't too small to allow air circulation, and as light weight as possible. Health officials stress malaria prevention more than treatment because treatment for the various strains is becoming quite complex. The word is out: Do not get bitten.

Careful hand washing is never more important than when traveling, just the time when it is often difficult if not impossible to accomplish. Carry a supply of packaged antiseptic towelettes (babywipes work well) in your day pack, plus a plastic ziplock bag with a small bar of soap and synthetic chamois mini-towel you can buy at a camping store.

Sunburn and sunstroke are two of the most common maladies requiring medical treatment while traveling. This is because UV rays are more harmful in some parts of the globe than in our own backyards, and also because some prescription medications make seniors' skin more sensitive. Don't forget to take a generous supply of sun block lotion, at least 15 SPF if you burn easily (it's expensive all over the world), a sun hat or two, sunglasses, and a water bottle. Constant sipping to prevent dehydration in hot climates is most important! And even if you don't normally wear sunglasses, you will need them while hiking the glaciers of New Zealand or sailing through the Greek islands. Ice and water glare are too powerful for naked eyesight to tolerate.

Medications, first-aid kit, eye wear

Travelers are often warned to keep prescribed maintenance drugs in their carry-on or day pack, yet there are repeated scenarios of lost or misplaced luggage containing vital cardiac or diabetic medications. Don't let this happen to you. Before departing, have up-to-date medical and dental checkups. Ask your doctor for typed copies of prescriptions with chemical names of drugs plus dosage, try to take enough medication with you for the whole trip (this may not be possible for a year's adventure), and keep the pills in their original containers in your day pack. Tell your pharmacist where you are going, and he or she may be able to pass on hints for refills, as well as package medications in lighter-weight containers. Don't repack pills yourself in order to save space or weight; customs officials may detain you for drug smuggling if what you are carrying is not officially identifiable. It has happened!

Miscellaneous prescription medications need to include a painkiller such as morphine or codeine, plus an antibiotic like Bactrim® or tetracycline for diarrhea or other infections encountered en route, such as an infected wound that requires more than topical treatment. And don't forget your antimalarials.

Nonprescribed medications to take along include antipyretics/ mild analgesics such as Tylenol® or aspirin (for fever, headache, sore throat, muscle pain), antihistamines such as Chlortripolon® or Benadryl® (for insect bites and stings, allergic reactions and sinus infections that require a decongestant prior to flying), Gravol® or Dramamine® for motion sickness or mild sedation, antidiarrhea medications such as Kaopectate®, Lomotil® or Imodium®, yogurt capsules and vitamins and rehydration packets such as Gastrolyte® or ORS which is packaged by WHO and available in most developing countries.

Basic first-aid kit requirements are simple. All you need is a plastic ziplock bag filled with: Band-Aids of various sizes, butterfly wound closures, one burn dressing, a piece of moleskin for blisters, a few cotton balls and Q-tips, small tubes of antibiotic topical ointment and Vaseline, throat lozenges, an antihistamine cream and/or aloe vera ointment for insect bites and sunburn, a tensor bandage, a one-ounce (30 mL) plastic bottle of 70% isopropyl alcohol or peroxide for cleansing wounds. You may want to add a sterile needle, and you should carry a pair of tweezers and scissors somewhere in your pack. When you're in the health food store purchasing yogurt capsules, pick up small containers of aloe vera ointment and arnica cream. My grandson calls my aloe vera ointment "Grandma's magic cream," as many fellow travelers have also discovered when I've passed it around for sunburn and bite treatment. Arnica cream rubbed into sore muscles gives almost instant relief; arnica tablets offer an herbal systemic anti-inflammatory as well. This hint was passed on to me from a fellow cyclist in Ireland — another joy of travel!

Adventure travel such as trekking, river rafting, altitudes over 10,000 feet (3,000 m), tropical snorkeling, or scuba diving or sailing requires special attention before you go. Equipping yourself with specific first-aid supplies plus knowledge of first-aid treatment for stings, bites, trauma and various fungal infections whether you are in the jungle or 19,000 feet up Mt. Kilimanjaro is a must, and demands specific research. High altitude sickness comes in three forms: Acute Mountain Sickness (AMS), High Altitude Pulmonary Edema (HAPE), and High Altitude Cerebral Edema (HACE). There are preventive measures with medication to start one to two days before ascent, acclimatizing routines to follow, and lots to know about it all. Read before you go, be physically ready for your adventure and allow more than enough preparation time. Consult your physician for altitude sickness prevention medication.

Lunchtime on the trail, Nepal

When I was severely stung by a man-of-war jelly fish while swimming in Tonga, I immediately applied aloe vera cream, then swallowed an antihistamine and mild analgesic. Within an hour I was pain-free with only a mildly raised welt from the tentacle that wrapped around my thigh. The welt continued until the next day; in the meantime I repeated the Chlortripolon® and acetaminophen which maintained my comfort, and I rubbed aloe vera into the welts. Both my husband, who has quite severe reactions to insect bites, and I do not travel without "Grandma's magic cream" plus over-the-counter antihistamines. Alcohol is also a topical antidote for jelly fish stings. It detoxifies the dangerous venom released by any clinging nematocysts which may be transferred to the skin from the tentacles. If you are going to be swimming in tropical waters, know first aid for poisonous stings, and have the appropriate supplies.

Another medical necessity is glasses. Take an old pair and your prescription along, just in case. Don't forget sunglasses, and use a head/neck retainer strap for active sports such as river rafting, or at all times if you are in the habit of taking your sunglasses on and off. I managed to preserve one expensive pair of sunglasses all the way around the world which I know wouldn't have happened if they weren't secured around my neck with a trusty black strap.

When traveling in developing countries, you need to take a small kit of sterile needles and syringes for emergency use by medical personnel. If you are unfortunate enough to require emergency treatment involving injections or intravenous therapy, you cannot rely on sterile technique anywhere outside of Western Europe and Australia and New Zealand. A point CDC's *Health Information for International Travel* stresses for international travelers is to establish a plan for dealing with medical emergencies. Having syringes and needles with you is part of Plan A. There are sterile kits pre-assembled and available for travelers through some travel agents (see "Appendix B" for mail order information), or travel clinics are usually prepared to supply you with a few basic syringes and needles with a covering note stating they are for emergency use only. Don't leave home without them if you are bound for Asia, India, Africa, or South America. And don't forget that the major cause for serious injury to international travelers is motor vehicle accidents. You won't find seat belts or safety-conscious drivers in most developing countries, so your risk ratio is high in two thirds of the world.

Perhaps the most important part of Plan A is to carry emergency assistance numbers, either IAMAT's (see "Appendix B" for addresses and phone numbers) list of English-speaking doctors or your credit card's toll-free number for world-wide hospital and doctor referrals. You also need to carry the addresses of your home country's consulates in the countries you will be visiting. The consulate will supply access to someone who can provide medical assistance; also, many international hotels have access to English-speaking doctors who, unfortunately, have a reputation for charging exorbitant fees. If your straits are not too dire and a hotel has offered to call a doctor for you, it may be prudent to ask about charges up front.

Plan B will center around what to do if: your partner is incapacitated; one or both of you dies; you are responsible for a rented vehicle that has been damaged or needs to be returned to the opposite side of a continent and you have been damaged; you are unable to cope with foreign emergency treatment and just want to get your sick or injured body home. Almost all of these predicaments are addressed somewhere in your insurance policies. Know the answers before you leave, and pass them on to your next of kin along with emergency instructions for them. Your son in Denver or Vancouver will not automatically know the intricacies of getting you safely home in a full body cast after he receives word that your back has been broken in a bus accident in northern Thailand. And preparing for these eventualities means they won't happen, right?

Last but not least, file all your health documents in a plastic ziplock bag. Include your health insurance policy and claim information, the phone numbers of English-speaking doctors from IAMAT plus consulate addresses, copies of medical prescriptions along with an eye glass prescription, and other insurance information regarding repatriation, return of vehicle, accompaniment for your travel partner—all of those emergency arrangements you don't want to think about.

The healthy traveler's checklist:

1) Preventive medicine

Q. What about immunizations and antimalaria medication?

check: with public health or travel clinic for immunization and antimalarial requirements and scheduling at least three months before travel time

Q. Where can I get accurate information regarding healthy travel?

check: "Appendix B" for addresses and phone numbers of US Department of Health and Human

Services Centers for Disease Control, the Canadian Public Health Association, the International Associations for Medical Assistance

check: "Appendix B" for mail order information for books: *Health Information for International Travel*, *Don't Drink the Water*, *The Pocket Doctor*

Q. What about the CDC hotline and IAMAT?

check: "Appendix B" for phone and fax numbers for obtaining these organizations' up-to-date travel information

Q. What do I need to treat traveler's diarrhea?

check: yogurt capsules, antibiotics prescribed by your doctor, antidiarrheals such as Imodium® or Lomotil® or Kaopectate®

Q. What about potable water in foreign lands?

check: water purifiers versus filters, iodine purification, boiling possibilities, availability of sealed bottled water

Q. What about jet lag?

check: time to acclimatize, being well rested, traveling westward

check: fluid intake, sleep sedative, library for diet and sleep and light regimes for overcoming jet lag

Q. What rest aides could I consider?

check: eye shields, mini cassette player, ear plugs

Q. What health aides are necessary?

check: insect repellent, matches or lighter for lighting mosquito coils, mosquito netting if recommended by the CDC or IAMAT, antiseptic towelettes, soap in a hand-washing kit, sun bloc, sun hat, sunglasses, water bottle

2) Medications, first-aid kit, eye wear

Q. Where do I pack medications I take every day?

check: carry-on or day pack, original containers

Q. What about medication supply?

check: enough digitalis, anticoagulants, insulin for whole trip, other prescription medication supplies

Q. What about prescription copies for medications and glasses?

check: legibility (typed), generic names, dosage, storage in plastic ziplock bag

Q. Do I need copy of ECG?

check: with physician for copy

Q. What miscellaneous prescription drugs do I need?

check: analgesics, antibiotics, antimalarials

Q. What nonprescription drugs do I need?

check: fever and mild pain killers, antihistamines, specific allergic reaction drugs if you require them, poisonous-sting antidotes, motion sickness pills, antidiarrhea medications, rehydration packets, vitamins, throat lozenges

Q. What do I need from the health food store?

check: yoghurt capsules, aloe vera ointment, arnica cream and tablets

Q. What goes into a basic first-aid kit?

check: Band-Aids of various sizes
wound closure steristrips
burn dressing
moleskin
cotton balls, Q-tips
antibiotic ointment
Vaseline

antihistamine, aloe vera cream
tensor bandage
alcohol or peroxide
sterile needle
tweezers, scissors

Q. *What extras should I think about?*

check: specifics for areas visiting, especially adventure travel including trekking, high altitude hiking, river rafting, snorkeling, scuba diving, sailing

Q. *What first-aid measures do I need to know?*

check: poisonous insect and snake bite treatment in areas where you will be traveling, especially marine animal hazards in tropical waters, altitude sickness treatment

Q. *What about eye wear?*

check: extra glasses, prescription, sunglasses, retaining straps

Q. *What happens if I need an emergency injection or intravenous treatment?*

check: supply of sterile needles and syringes

Q. *How do I deal with medical emergencies?*

check: establishing Plan A with sterile supplies, list of English-speaking doctors, consulate addresses

check: establishing Plan B with procedures for incapacitated travel, repatriation, accompaniment for incapacitated travel partner, return of vehicle, insurance coverage, emergency instruction to next of kin

Q. *Where do I keep health documents?*

check: ziplock bag for insurance policy, claim information, medicine and eye glass prescriptions, addresses and phone numbers

Chapter Seven

Money Matters

How to get it: bank machines, credit cards, traveler's checks

Travel financing in today's electronic age is much easier than it was in our youth, or even ten years ago. While it's not difficult to recognize the current realities of increased population and choking pollution, plus increased risks in travel security, slotting a plastic card from North America into a machine in Istanbul that spits out Turkish money so one can purchase a real carpet seems like pure magic. Pull out a card and a genie appears, ready to buy anything your heart desires.

Which is one of the disadvantages, of course. We have to hold onto our magic cards while keeping our budget in sight in these days of easy money. Assuming you can focus on your own spending limits, I will attempt to outline the general concepts of international banking and traveler's checks.

Major credit cards such as VISA and MasterCard allow you

Open-air carpet market, Mugla, Turkey

to withdraw cash advances from banks anywhere in the world that display their sign. Sometimes you can use automatic teller machines (ATMs), but you can't always count on them. You have to get to know the territory. In Turkey, for instance, some banks work better than others while some cards will not work at all from an ATM that bears their insignia; you have to go through the inside teller which means doing your banking during regular hours. If you arrive penniless at a small Turkish port on the Aegean coast on Sunday morning, you may have to hunt for a bank machine that accepts your card, or resort to using your emergency supply of US-dollar traveler's checks to get you through until the banks open on Monday. When you get to a larger city with more choice, you can try out the different banking machines until you find one that works for your card, complete with instructions in English.

Your bank card allows you to use an ATM anywhere in the world that displays the signs imprinted on the card: Cirrus, Plus and Interac are the major networks. Before you leave, check with your home bank that your PIN (personal identification number) will be recognized internationally; some institutions issue an altered number for international ATMs. Also check with your home bank about foreign availability of ATMs displaying your insignia. Be specific about your destinations.

Credit cards charge for each international cash advance (usually one or two dollars) plus interest on the amount withdrawn calculated within a thirty or sixty day period or whenever you pay the balance. Most bank cards also charge for international transactions, but there are no interest charges. And with your bank card you get the best of all possible exchange rates because they are based on wholesale foreign currency buying by your bank. Avoid unnecessary bank charges when taking too little too often. Withdraw what you are comfortable with in your money belt, and try not to retrace your steps to the bank every other day.

If relying solely on a bank card in areas where you are absolutely confident that it will work, remember that your bank account must stand the assault of continuous cash withdrawals. As I have noted in the chapter "Before You Leave: Business details" (page 82), discuss your travel plans with the bank manager (get a business card with the fax number of the bank) and make sure there will be enough money in your account or line of credit to cover outstanding balances or emergency withdrawals. Do not travel on such a tight budget that you have no maneuverability for emergencies or a splurge — it's not fun. Maybe you needed to travel under those conditions when you were twenty, but a few grey hairs and wrinkles mean you can relax and enjoy the world; you are now experiencing some things for the only time. I doubt I will get the chance to return to Tanzania for another wildlife safari, but I will never forget falling asleep to the rhythmic chomping of Cape buffaloes as they wrenched clumps of grass from around my tent. And I learned the hard way that Tanzania is not wired into international banking, and that I didn't have enough US-dollar traveler's checks to cover my expenses. But I had a fabulous time, and luckily my fellow safari members

Cape Buffalo at a safe distance, Tanzania

had enough extra cash to treat me to an occasional *Tusker* (the local beer).

Bank cards and ATMs and credit cards are great for those parts of the world connected to international banking systems; in developing countries you still have to rely on good old traveler's checks to safely see you through your adventures. And in some very rural places that don't take kindly to traveler's checks, you will have to have cash — in the local currency, of course. But you don't want to carry any more cash than is absolutely necessary, so traveler's checks remain a necessity. Purchasing them as you go means you will probably pay the highest commission fee at a bank, no fee at American Express if you have an AMEX card, and no fee at a Thomas Cook office. Buy as much as you can before leaving home; most likely your bank will have a fee-free program with Visa or MasterCard.

Cashing traveler's checks can cost either a percentage of the amount cashed, a flat fee, or nothing. If you can change $10 or $100 for the same fee, obviously you will save if you change in one transaction as much as you can safely carry; cashing at a branch of the traveler's-check-issuing company such as American Express or Thomas Cook will cost you nothing; cashing at a bank instead of a hotel or business will get you a better rate than the hotel or business will charge. Remember to get some low denomination cash. Taxi drivers and shop merchants don't like to change big bills for small charges, and in fact may refuse to do so.

Lost or stolen traveler's checks will not be replaced by the issuing company without a copy of the purchase agreement — that fine print form you sign when you buy the checks. Carry the agreement separately from the checks, and try to keep track of what you have used. If your money belt does disappear, you need to know how many traveler's checks you have lost. Phone the number listed in the agreement, and follow the company's instructions for replacement. Just like credit cards, the sooner you phone the less you will be responsible for in the replacement scheme. Like American Express and their own traveler's checks, Thomas Cook is now affiliated with MasterCard which uses several Hertz branch offices as well. If you lose MasterCard traveler's checks, phone (609) 987-7300, collect, from anywhere in the world.

Traveler's checks can be obtained in most major currencies before leaving home. Japanese yen, French francs, German deutschemarks are all available from your local bank; Dominican Republic pesos probably will not be. With minor currencies it is advisable to take traveler's checks in US dollars plus some US cash to exchange for local currency as soon as you arrive. Take some small denominations for quick exchange at the airport if your arrival time is after banking hours, and head for the bank the next day. If you are traveling to "strong-currency countries" such as France or Australia, you might consider buying the major portion of you foreign currency traveler's checks as soon as possible in your planning stage, knowing that they will probably get more expensive as time goes by. Obviously, the converse is true for "weak-currency countries" such as Mexico or Turkey where the cost will probably be cheaper if you wait until you arrive. Of course, none of these predictions by money experts are absolutely certain, so you are taking a calculated risk. Another way to check is to watch the daily exchange rates published in major newspapers. After a short time, you can get a basic idea of what is happening on the money markets. Whatever you decide, arrange

High in the Austrian Alps

for at least a small amount of foreign currency — both cash and traveler's checks — if it is available, before you go. Allow the bank enough time, at least a week or two.

If you are vagabonding around the world, you won't want to collect money for each country before you go. You can usually buy money near a border. Regardless of all the warnings about exchanging money on the street or through the black market, at times you have no choice, and instant exchanges become a matter of going with the flow. Usually there is someone to advise you; a bus driver will say yes or no, sometimes obviously, sometimes covertly. Watch for signs, ask other travelers, change only enough to get you to a bank, and keep your reserves well hidden.

Carrying a reserve of US-dollar traveler's checks is a very reassuring way to travel. You know you can always cash them, you won't have to overpurchase local currency and then pay another exchange fee to get rid of it (if you miscalculate locally, you have your US-dollar backup), and you won't have to rely on an emergency credit card advance that may be impossible to obtain. Given that your US-dollar traveler's checks have been purchased fee-free through your bank, Thomas Cook or American

Express, they are the least expensive way to go. For more on traveling with American dollars, see "Comfort: Planning a mature traveler's budget," page 14. Try to keep some low denomination traveler's checks as well as higher amounts. Plan ahead for purchasing any and all traveler's checks — major centers are sometimes few and far between in developing countries, and it may be very difficult to get money if you find yourself broke or in need of emergency funding.

Where foreign banking facilities appear to be less than modern as far as electronics are concerned, it is still possible to wire money. And sometimes it is the most expedient way to receive a lump sum. When we rented a farm house in expensive, picturesque Tuscany, our California-born landlady was genuinely surprised to hear that her local bank wired a "help message" to our bank in Canada and received the requested cash within twenty-four hours. She was used to Italian red tape and a bureaucracy that accomplishes most things at a snail's pace, in spite of a frantic façade. Our biggest difficulty was getting the bank personnel to slow down enough to grasp our hesitant Italian. Aiutare! (help!) finally was understood.

Credit and travel cards: how many, which ones, lost or stolen

Each credit and travel card company has its own idiosyncrasies. Keep in mind that the companies are highly competitive, then pursue your research. Some important points for consideration are: annual fees including costs for supplementary cards; spending limits; air miles or points earned (which airlines, if it makes a difference); emergency card replacement procedures; when interest charges occur (some only after sixty days); world-wide travel assistance with emergency phone numbers; mail service; rental car insurance coverage (CDW) and in what countries; other travel insurance coverage such as trip cancellation, loss of baggage, flight delay or medical; hotel reservation hotlines; stipulations for benefit coverage (whether or not purchased with card); financial services such as personal check cashing; cost of traveler's checks; cost of cash advances.

Lost or stolen credit cards are handled according to the particular procedures of each individual card. There is no central emergency number for all VISA cards; each banking institution has its own. MasterCard's international collect number to be called from anywhere in the world is (314) 275-6690. Individual travel companies like American Express or Diners Club have their own toll-free or collect numbers to call internationally. The more cards you carry, the more telephone numbers you need to have with you, and the more vulnerable you are to financial difficulties if any or all cards disappear from your possession.

You *must* report a missing card as soon as possible. The small print of your card holder agreement will tell you the amount of charges you are responsible for in the interim between when the card is missing and reporting time; the amount for my Canadian VISA card is $50. But don't wait a day or two thinking you have just misplaced your card and that it will surface somewhere in your luggage. Even if it does reappear in your possession, you are better to report it missing as soon as you can't find it so that you are not liable for unauthorized or illegal debt if it really is being misused. If and when the original does resurface, cut it into at least two pieces and discard the pieces immediately. And you already know to never leave your card(s) behind while you are off adventuring or on a mini-tour.

Most card companies now have fairly quick replacement services, but whether you are in London or Kathmandu, a missing card can be a major upheaval in your travel plans. Replacement credit cards are usually reissued through your home banking institution and then couriered to you, so you may wait more than the card company's estimated twenty-four hours to get a new one in your hands. A few years ago you would have had to return home to get a new credit card, but this is changing.

American Express offers world-wide emergency card replacement usually by the end of the next business day, but American Express travel cards are not truly credit cards in the same sense as banking institution cards. However, American Express does have an ancillary Optima Card which is purchased as a companion to one of AMEX's other cards for $15 a year, and used as a bank card that charges to your AMEX account rather than withdrawing from your bank. Optima card use costs $2 for each transaction plus 1 percent of the amount advanced, so each $300 cash advance will cost $5. AMEX has a new Green Credit Card which will access Interac ATMs in Canada. Optima cards are necessary for accessing Interac in the US and Europe (information current in 1995). Both the Green Credit Card and Optima are valid only for Interac ATMs — they will not work for over-the-counter banking like VISA and MasterCards (wherever their signs are displayed). AMEX does have its own banking system through its own branch offices around the world, so you can travel everywhere on just an American Express travel card provided you use it to get money at AMEX offices where you can cash personal checks and buy fee-free traveler's checks. When I traveled around the world for eight months, this is how I obtained a continuous supply of money. An added plus was being able to reliably receive mail. See "Comfort: Planning a mature traveler's budget" on page 14 for more on American Express.

A Diners Club or En Route card is similar to American Express in that it is a travel card. VISA and MasterCard are credit cards issued by financial companies that have memberships in most banking institutions around the world. VISA is probably the most widely accepted by both banks and merchants. All the major cards — VISA, MasterCard, American Express, Diners — participate in frequent flyer point programs, and all are highly competitive with other benefits. Credit cards are more acceptable than travel cards at home for charging and accumulating airline points. A year's supply of groceries plus a bathroom renovation will probably earn a free flight to Europe. I was pleased when American Express transferred my Canadian Airline points from AMEX to my VISA Canadian frequent flyer program, thereby consolidating and letting me continue to earn points when buying my groceries.

Read all the fine print before deciding which cards to take with you. If you are traveling in developed countries, you may want to tote your bank card in conjunction with a travel or credit card. Both travel cards and credit cards have distinct and different advantages. Which ones you need depends on where you are going. If you get stuck in Florence on a holiday weekend with no money and the AMEX office closed, you can probably access an ATM with a credit card. If you get stuck in Arusha with no money, no cards will help, and you will have to wire home for funds. Remember that a credit card will have more access to over-the-counter banking than a travel card. If you are traveling in less developed areas of the world, you may as well leave your bank card at home, and use either your travel or credit card for purchases as well as banking wherever possible. When I ran out of money in Tanzania, the bank refused a cash advance on my VISA card (this had nothing to do with cash limits; they simply were not part of the system for any credit card), but finally, after much persuasion, the manager allowed me to write a personal check for $100 — and that was all. I didn't miss my safari connection, and the $100 turned out to be enough to keep me in bottled water during safari plus tip the guides at the end.

Charging whatever you can directly onto a credit card has the obvious advantage of allowing you to carry less cash, but often stores and tourist businesses build-in a service charge for credit card use, usually 1 or 2 percent of the amount charged. Some travelers strongly object to this; I consider it a trade for flying points. Also, many — in fact most — small hotels and guest houses do not take credit cards for payment so you will need cash when you are traveling independently. Before you decide how many and which cards to take, study your itinerary to see which ones you can actually use, and leave the rest at home. Don't forget to take your frequent flyer card for use at airport check-ins, your telephone calling card, and your OAP card — in British Columbia, Canada it's a Gold Card — to flash for senior's discounts. You will need little else, and you will not turn your trip into a nightmare if your cards disappear.

Antiques made to order, Ubud, Bali

Another advantage to having a readily acceptable, multipurpose card with you in developed countries is that you may be able to use it for medical emergency funding if payment is required before treatment is given. Hospitals may accept a credit card in lieu of cash after they determine there is a high enough limit on the card to afford them some security, or you may have to obtain a large amount of cash advance from a bank to cover hospital or ambulance charges or other costs of returning yourself or your travel partner home unexpectedly. Make sure large cash advances are possible, and raise your limits before you go to cover emergencies, then be extra cautious about the use of your card while traveling — watch when it is imprinted, and don't ever leave it as security for a borrowed or rented article. It won't have much value in developing countries that don't subscribe to the system, but more developed tourist-wise areas have learned how to use cards illegally without compunction.

Some travelers like to spread their charges across different credit card accounts, using one for travel expenses, another for purchases, keeping a third for emergencies. They will also keep cards in separate places for security reasons, and also keep multiple limits low as a safety precaution. I think this is unnecessary juggling, and I don't recommend it as a safe way to travel. Check your debt responsibility clause, and purchase credit card insurance coverage if you want extra assurance. And don't forget — you have to pay for all of those cards.

Another rather obscure use for a credit card is for VAT refunds. Shopping in Europe and bringing goods home to North America allows you to claim a country's value-added tax — as high as 20 percent in Sweden and Denmark. Ask for a tax-free shopping check when you buy (the sales clerks fill in your passport number and other information), get the check stamped by customs as you exit the country with the goods, and either collect cash from a Tax Free for Tourists booth near the customs station, or mail the stamped document back to the store who will refund it on your credit card, or mail you a check, or deposit the refund in your bank account.

The easiest way to obtain the refund is at a Tax Free for Tourists window, but you may then be stuck with foreign cash that you don't want. However you claim the VAT, it isn't difficult, and refunds do happen. I have received a check (in my home currency) in the mail, and also have had deposits made to my bank account within a few weeks of my mailing the stamped receipts back to the store. Shop personnel are careful when doing the documentation and it only takes a moment or two, but they seldom offer you the refund option. You have to ask for it. The reason it isn't refunded immediately is because countries have limits before refunds happen; sometimes it's $50, sometimes it's $200, usually stated in local currency which is less affected by fluctuating foreign exchange rates. In Italy, for example, if you spend over 300,000 Italian lire (Cdn$270) in a shop, you will be refunded 11.5 percent to 16 percent IVA, the amount depending on the type of goods purchased.

In some countries VAT refund companies compete with each other, but no matter how you are lured to use a specific refund system, the basic procedure of filling in the documentation when you buy, and then having it stamped by customs upon exit is the same. How you collect is your choice; even if you've bought just a few items, it is worth it.

The money matters checklist:

1) How to get it

Q. How do I get a cash advance on my credit card?

check: for credit card sign at bank or ATM, inside teller if machine doesn't work, banking hours, with home bank for international availability of card use (be specific regarding your destinations)

Q. Can I use my bank card in foreign countries?

check: international availability of ATMs identical to signs on your card, with home bank regarding international recognition of your PIN (it may need to be altered), adequate funds in your account

Q. What fees do I pay to use credit and bank cards?

check: credit card transaction charges for international cash advance and interest charges, bank card international transaction charges

Q. What pre-trip financial arrangements should I complete?

check: discussion of travel plans with bank, which cards to use where, budget maneuverability, funding for cash withdrawals or advance payments

check: foreign banking services through travel card companies such as American Express, Diners Club

Q. How do I get money in countries not connected to international electronic banking systems?

check: availability of traveler's checks centers (American Express and Thomas Cook or bank), travel supply of personal checks if using AMEX or other foreign banking services, wire services, telex, Western Union

Q. How do I have money wired to me?

check: fax and phone numbers of home bank or person who can wire money through local bank or telex office

Q. What if my traveler's checks are stolen or lost?

check: traveler's check agreement carried separate from checks, list of checks used, phone number to call if traveler's checks missing, replacement procedure of issuing company or bank

Q. What does it cost to buy and cash traveler's checks?

check: commission fees at banks and traveler's check companies (American Express, Thomas Cook) when buying at home and on the road, commissions charged to cash (usually the lowest at banks, nothing at AMEX or Thomas Cook/MasterCard if traveler's checks purchased from them)

Q. Can I purchase foreign currency in North America?

check: home bank for major foreign currency cash and traveler's checks, speciality exchange banks in large centers for smaller countries' cash or traveler's checks

Q. What is the best backup money to carry?

check: US-dollar traveler's checks and US cash, increased credit card limits for emergency funds

Q. What are some tips for buying foreign currency at home?

check: small as well as large denominations, strong or weak currency countries, when to buy

Q. How do I get money when entering a country and there are no banks near the border?

check: on-the-street exchanges by the locals, ask local advice, change smallest amount possible

2) Credit and travel cards

Q. What about travel and credit card idiosyncrasies?

check: annual fees, spending limits, airline points, emergency card replacement procedures, when interest is charged, travel assistance programs, rental car insurance coverage including which countries, travel insurance, financial services, cost of traveler's checks and cash advances

Q. What if my travel or credit card is missing?

check: lost or stolen procedures for each card, phone numbers to call when missing, amount of your liability for illegal use of card

Q. What is the difference between a credit card and a travel card?

check: compare individual company travel cards such as American Express, Diners Club or Carte Blanche with banking institution credit cards such as VISA: emergency replacement, ATM use, charge card use for travel versus charge card for home use, travel services offered including personal check cashing and mail services, financial services offered including traveler's checks, personal check cashing, and cash advances, emergency funding if lost or stolen

Q. How do I decide which cards to take with me?

check: the fine print, where you are going, what financial services are available for which cards, what travel services are available for which cards

Q. What charge card advantages should I look for?

check: need for cash, service charges for credit and travel card purchases, emergency funding availability

Q. Should I raise my limits?

check: emergency funding available, travel needs using one card versus multiple cards

Q. What about VAT?

check: tax-free shopping receipt when purchasing, customs stamp when exiting country with goods, methods of refund: credit card, bank account, check, cash

Chapter Eight

As You Go

Going with the flow while learning to say no

For many North Americans, saying no is difficult. We are afraid of offending others or of missing something beneficial to our well-being. Learning how to say no to pestering touts without sounding negative, or learning how to reject unmetered taxi drivers while searching for a metered one requires alertness and patience. The biggest problem with finding the best solution for your immediate needs is that most of the people who want to serve you know that high-pressure, hurry-up tactics are effective. "You come, come with me, I give you best price ... how much you pay, buy my peanuts, they are best ... take my taxi, I same as meters" ... it goes on and on ... until you give in. It is disconcerting, and it may also be costly, especially when you learn later that the taxi you accepted under pressure charged twice as much as the authorized fare.

Seasoned travelers often become brusque and hardened to

Out of the Bible, into the wheat fields, Turkey

demands by locals, but remembering that most everyone responds positively to a smile — even when saying no — can make life easier. Letting the taxi driver know you are not going to make a snap decision, and that you are going to remain calm, automatically brings the price down. Pestering vendors on the beach in Mexico are best treated with a firm nod of the head, a pleasant facial expression, and no eye contact. Some Turks can get more than a little irate if you accept their invitation to a glass of tea and then do not buy; others say "no problem" and they genuinely mean it. Take the time to feel the atmosphere. Is it high pressure "come and buy only from me right now," or is it "I would like to help you if you will let me?" After traveling in Indonesia where most services are bargained for under pressure, I had to be reminded in more relaxed Turkey to "smile and be happy." I had so hardened myself to high-pressure tactics that I couldn't accept a friendly offer of a glass of local apple tea. When I finally did let down my defenses, I was treated to a private tour by a Sufi scholar of Konya's Museum of the Whirling Dervishes along with an invitation to an academic Whirling Dervish dance performance (they are illegal otherwise) being staged for a group from the University of Southern California. Unfortunately, I couldn't attend the dance performance because of travel commitments, but if I had remained aloof and uncommunicative, I would have missed my special museum tour plus a lot more of Turkey.

It's true that touts and vendors are more insistent in heavily trafficked tourist areas, such as the old-city section of Istanbul. This is when you have to get to know the atmosphere: is it best to say a firm no, ignore altogether, bargain if you feel like it, be up-front by saying "yes, I would like to look at a carpet museum, but I am not going to buy," or let it be known that you might be interested in making a purchase? Bargaining is often a cultural tradition, and in many countries you will be expected to behave like the locals when shopping. This can be tedious and take time you might not want to spare in order to quickly purchase a Mexican serape or a Balinese carving before leaving the country. More and more cooperative craft stores (baskets, jewelery, pottery, carvings) and factory shops (silk, leather, batik) with fixed prices are being established in tourist centers around the world. Check the quality and prices before buying; there is always an unbiased source of knowledge somewhere — in your hotel, at the visitor's center, in guidebooks describing specialities of a region. If you want to buy a carpet in Turkey, read about carpets and kilims before you go, and perhaps visit an import carpet dealer in your home town. Being knowledgeable about anything relieves anxiety, and this is never more true than when traveling. The more you learn about a new culture you want to experience, the easier it will be to go with the flow. You may spend a few unnecessary dollars in the beginning, but when you can relax and still say no — or yes — you will be a happy traveler.

Getting around: money, transportation, accommodation, food, language

The first thing you need is money — you can't go anywhere or do anything without it. You have landed in a strange country at two o'clock in the morning, faced with a foreign language and a strange currency. The airport exchange windows are closed, there are no local money changers on the street, the train and bus stations are deserted. Hopefully, you have enough local currency to last until banking hours, or you have a low denomination traveler's check to cash at the hotel to pay your taxi, and previous research has prepared you for obtaining a further supply of cash when the banks open.

A taxi driver kindly delivers you to his brother-in-law's pension which looks clean and comfortable, and certainly is affordable. Morning comes all too soon, but a stunning view of the shimmering Mediterranean lapping the beach three hundred feet below your balcony must mean that you have arrived at the right place. A breakfast tray appears with coffee, fresh rolls, a little goat cheese, some olives and sliced tomatoes ... are you in paradise?

So far this is more than you bargained for; you thought you might get stuck in some run-down guesthouse next to the train station for a night or two, then find suitable accommodation for a week or more. Things were hectic at home, and spending the first few days of your trip in a major city (where you had hotel reservations) wasn't very restful. Yet, here you are, settled in the place of your dreams. Now you can concentrate on the local scene, learn some foreign language phrases, and just ... relax.

Is this scenario a fantasy, something that happens only in books? Not so for many travelers. While goat cheese and olives are not standard breakfast fare in every country, one can rely on taxi drivers around the world to find a room that is surprisingly comfortable and inexpensive. And remember that many towns and most cities have tourist information centers. Don't be afraid to use them.

Ask where the locals like to eat. In developing countries follow the rules about fresh produce and dairy and meat products. You may get tired of noodles or rice or rice or noodles in Asia, but stay on the safe side. Chicken is a reliable source of protein when it is well cooked. Do not eat fish that you can't "see the head and tail on your plate" (large fish can harbor poisonous toxins), and never eat any kind of raw shellfish, including ceviche which is marinated shellfish. India is a great place for vegetarians who like curried vegetables.

Local transportation can be anything from a camel to a cable car, as exotic as *felucca* sailing down the Nile or cycling the tow

The oldest form of transportation, Lindos, Greece

paths along French canals in early morning mist. Whether you are on a ski lift or a sail boat, be aware of safety. Check for life preservers, and make sure you have a map of unfamiliar ski terrain. In developing countries, it may be part of the local experience to ride a public bus, but seemingly suicidal drivers can convince one to spend a few more cents for a private bus going in the same direction at a slower and safer speed. Use caution and common sense when using public transportation. If you insist on riding the roof of an incredibly overcrowded train from Bombay to Calcutta, you are definitely traveling at your own risk.

When you are preparing for airport departure from a country, check the amount of departure tax and in what currency it must be paid. Also check about exchanging leftover local money before you leave; many countries will give only a partial refund, usually twenty or thirty percent of cash, and you may be left with useless money once you are over the border. Some countries will also require proof that you have legally exchanged money in their country, so save your exchange slips from the bank until you have left the country.

Foreign language opportunities abound, but unfortunately for many travelers, speaking another language is the most inhibiting aspect of travel. One of the best ways to overcome "communication terror" is to take a language course; skill in the basics can be acquired in just a few weeks of classes, or you can learn at your own pace with any of the cassette courses that are sold in the travel sections of bookstores or through mail order. They can also be borrowed from your local library. Greek, Portuguese, Russian, Turkish, Arabic, Bahassa Indonesian or Malaysian, Mandarin Chinese, Japanese, Thai ... the list seems infinite. Just a few hours of listening to a tape will help you feel comfortable with strange sounds, and taking the tape along to review while traveling, using your mini-cassette player, is always a boost.

A pocket dictionary or local phrase book is an essential piece of baggage. Most language courses come with their own or you can buy them separately. Berlitz, Cortina, Living Language, Linguaphone all publish language courses and dictionaries. Rick Steves' phrase books are highly recommended by many independent travelers; see "Appendix A" for mail-order address.

Don't be intimidated by a different language. It is all part of experiencing another culture, and you may be pleasantly surprised by how relaxed the locals are with you in spite of your foreign sounds.

It is always helpful to know how to count, especially when buying goods or exchanging currency. If you are completing a business deal or making travel arrangements, make sure you understand what is happening. Verify all amounts and travel times; a slight misunderstanding could cost in terms of travel time or money.

Worldly connections: fax, phone, telex, mail

If credit cards are the magic carpets of our electronic age, fax machines represent the Rolls-Royce of twentieth century worldwide communications. Telephone cables and international circuits specifically designed for fax calls provide the necessary means for

Balinese sales girls, Indonesia

data communications that defy the cost plus the static and audible interruptions of voice communication. Faxes almost always get through, even if it is 3:00 A.M. on the other side of the planet. They can be used for emergency messages as well as travel journal updates — and every country has one somewhere.

Interconnecting computer systems connect humans to humans wherever computer communication systems exist, which can be few and far between in developing countries. Sending a letter E-mail from Nairobi to New York remains a possibility for the future.

Besides facsimile machines, there is still the good old telephone. Callers from North America traveling in almost any country in the world can connect to an English-speaking operator (plus French for Canadians) within seconds. Canadians can call Canada using the Canada Direct service which charges Canadian rates (usually lower than overseas long distance rates) to either their calling card or HELLO! Phone Pass, or collect calls to Canada only. Canada Direct will also connect a caller to other countries, but this service may be more expensive than direct country-to-country dialing because there is a charge for the first leg to Canada, plus the second country-to-country leg. Charges on calls to Canada are based on time of day in Canada, so a call received after 5 P.M. or before 8 A.M. may be a convenient and cheap time to phone from Europe. HELLO! Phone Passes are purchased before you go for $10, $20, $50, or $100. (They make a nice gift to a grandchild on a grand tour, and perhaps save on collect calls.) Canada Direct access numbers and dialing codes are listed in *Bon Voyage, But*, see "Appendix A" for address, or contact your telephone company. Remember that hotels like to add surcharges for any phone use, so check before making even a Canada Direct collect call; you may have to use your calling card from a public pay phone. Americans using Sprint, MCI, or AT&T cards connect to US Direct through their phone company's calling card (plus a PIN for some cards). Sprint has connections in 250 countries, and adds an $.80 surcharge per call. Check with your calling card company for US Direct numbers, codes, and charges, and don't forget to take them with you.

If you prefer to make a direct call (without an English-speaking intermediary), you can insert your credit card into the phone in some countries (Australia and New Zealand are great for this), or buy a local card exchanging so much coin for so many minutes in a phone box, usually at a post office. If you can't or don't want to use your credit card or cash, your phone company calling card is a travel necessity. Don't leave home without it.

When you are making any kind of call from a hotel room phone, check with the desk about hotel surcharges. You may have to insist on an accurate answer, not just "yes, there is a charge" — the amount of which can be staggering. European hotels especially can charge as much as $10 just to connect you with an operator. Purchasing phone cards for use in public phone boxes

Punting on the River Avon, Christchurch, New Zealand

is most common in Europe and Mediterranean countries, but it truly tries your patience when a $10 card doesn't work and you have waited until after the issuing store's hours to connect with home at the proper time. So beware — in some places, the cards are not reliable; if you go through a post office, the system usually works.

Believe it or not, telegrams, telexes, and moneygrams still have a place in our high-tech world of electronic communications. As you travel, you will notice that wire services are most visible in developing countries. American Express offers a moneygram service if you don't have a personal check to cash. If you are thousands of miles from an AMEX office, Western Union can wire and receive money, and most banks have a telex. Whether it's an emergency call for medical help or money, wire services can do it, so don't despair if you can't get through on a phone or fax. Look for Western Union.

Mail while you are traveling can be a necessary nuisance or a welcome relief. However you view it, before you leave let your correspondents know when and where to send mail to you. American Express and Thomas Cook will give you addresses of their offices around the world, and there is always General Delivery or Post Restante in major centers. American Express is a reliable service for members, and they will generally hold mail for thirty days. Thomas Cook has a few more regulations for holding mail; consult your local Thomas Cook or affiliate office for their particulars. I was warned by friends who live in Indonesia not to trust the mail system there, and sure enough, my daughter's Christmas card with photo of my newborn grandson that she risked sending to my hotel in Bali was opened "by mistake" by the hotel staff before I received it.

In many developing countries, outgoing mail is just as risky as incoming correspondence. The only sure way of getting anything into or out of India or Nepal is to take it yourself, so tell your friends not to expect to hear from you while you are there. And everyone knows of postcards arriving home from anywhere in the world after the sender returns. If it is going to be necessary to make business contacts from a questionable destination, try to determine how to do so before you leave: if fax will be the best way, make sure you have necessary fax numbers; if telephoning is the most convenient, establish a date and time range to receive your calls, and if you must receive mail, find a reliable address wherever you will be, either a hotel or AMEX or Thomas Cook office.

Emergencies: if you are sick or hurt, or are missing any of the Three Essentials

The International Association for Medical Assistance to Travelers (IAMAT) is a voluntary organization that provides access to emergency medical care around the world. The organization coordinates the services of doctors who subscribe to IAMAT's standards as well as their fee schedules, and who either speak English or another language in addition to their native tongue. To become a member of IAMAT and receive their list of clinics world-wide, phone or write IAMAT, 40 Regal Road, Guelph, Ontario N1K 1B5, phone (519) 836-0102, or 417 Center Street, Lewiston, New York 14092, phone (716) 754-4883. Fees for IAMAT's medical services need to be paid upon receipt of service; insurance claims can then be filed for reimbursement.

It is very reassuring to know there is quality medical service available in most developing countries; nevertheless, certain precautions are recommended. Carry a medical emergency kit of sterile syringes and needles (see "The Healthy Traveler," page 100), your own supply of digitalis, anticoagulants, and insulin if you require them, have a typed prescription for other continuous drugs stating the trade name, manufacturer's and chemical name of the drug plus the dosage, carry a recent copy of your electrocardiogram if you have a heart condition, and, without fail, have a list of your allergies and an allergy bracelet.

Look in guidebooks or travel publications for foreign embassy addresses of your home country (or ask your home consulate for addresses), and make note of them before you leave. Canadian embassies are listed in *Bon Voyage, But,* a government publication by the Department of Foreign Affairs and International Trade (see "Appendix A" for mail order address). Americans can obtain a copy of the US State Department's *Key Officers of Foreign Service Posts* (see "Appendix A" for mail order address). If you need medical help in a strange land, your consulate can advise you, and they will assist if you are hurt or a victim of crime. They will not replace missing traveler's checks, but they will help with replacing a lost or stolen passport and possibly a visitor's visa. You are not alone when visiting a foreign country, and if you need help, don't hesitate to call on your embassy. Assisting their fellow countrymen is an embassy's *raison d'être* — a fact often obscured by political and social protocol.

Report a missing passport to your nearest embassy immediately; most consulates have a twenty-four-hour phone line. Having

Treats on Lovuka Island, Fiji

several extra photos and a photocopy of your passport signature page will expedite replacement, but you will have a few hours to a few days wait, depending on where you are.

Lost or stolen traveler's checks are replaced according to the company's agreement that comes with the checks. Keeping the agreement separate from the checks is one precaution; photocopying and leaving a copy with a responsible person at home is another. If you are in a major center, the checks can be replaced soon after you have called the toll-free refund number to file a claim. Even if you are in an outpost far from banks, checks can be wired through Western Union. If you're further out than any kind of telecommunications, you will have to wait. But don't forget to obtain the police report with the date of theft clearly stated.

Follow your credit card instructions for getting emergency replacement if a card is lost or stolen; have the phone numbers handy. See "Money Matters: Credit cards" on page 111 for more on replacement.

Report any missing tickets to the issuer and the police as soon as possible. RailEurope will reimburse for theft or accidental loss of RailPasses, but the pass holder must purchase replacements in the meantime — the same goes for airline tickets. Check lost or stolen ticket replacement procedures before you leave. You will need a copy of the police report to go with your claim form which you can usually file upon returning home.

When traveling, keep your emergency information together in a ziplock plastic bag: who to notify in case of emergency, your lawyer's business card, emergency replacement numbers for credit and travel cards and traveler's checks, IAMAT membership cards and foreign addresses of clinics, medical and travel insurance documents including medical evacuation instructions, other medical service numbers provided by your insurance policies and credit cards, your international vaccination certificate, embassy addresses, medical and eyewear prescriptions, ... and anything else pertinent to safe travel. It's handy to have a calendar page of the months you are traveling attached to your itinerary because it's easy to lose track of days, especially important if you are on a timed cycle of medication. All of these bits and pieces don't require much space or time to gather, and once you have your packet of emergency information, you will feel more secure about experiencing those interesting, but at times intimidating, developing countries.

Rest and respite

Traveling can be exhausting. If you let yourself get too tired, just when you need to have your wits about you, your decision-making capabilities are impaired. Or you get sick, or hurt. Or you blow your cool.

Take time to recover after a long journey; allow yourself time to catch up when you have crossed several time zones. Develop ways to orient yourself to a new area. Use the map from your hotel for a walk around the neighbourhood (after you have a nap). Your own sense of direction will keep you oriented during your stay. Small towns or villages throughout Europe are built around a central square or piazza which is probably where your accommodation will be located. Walk the central district, find the churches, and locate restaurants that are close to your hotel. Allow enough time for a walk and a rest if needed. Have a drink in the local watering hole, and don't lose sight of the reason for

Aegean coast fishing village, Gümüşluk, Turkey

your trip which is to learn about and understand a culture different from your own and to have fun.

Extensive, continuous travel can numb the senses; traveling in Southeast Asia can be a succession of open sewers, fried noodles, and tortuously loud rock and roll until we take time to notice the natives placing fruit and bamboo offerings in spirit houses, or visit a butterfly farm. But if we are so tired that we sleep through the scenery and shrug our shoulders at the butterflies, we may as well be home taking a nap.

Continuous travel over several weeks or months calls for frequent breaks, so plan for this in your itinerary. Searching for an apartment to set up a brief stint of housekeeping opens up the local scene, but can be frustrating as well as rewarding. After renting (before we left home) a renovated seventeenth century farmhouse for a week in Tuscany, we tried, on-the-spot, to lease an apartment for a few days on the Amalfi coast in Italy, but were unable to find anything habitable. A few years later we were pleasantly rewarded with an on-the-spot search in Turkey where we spent an exquisite, restful week in an apartment in a tiny fishing village on the Aegean coast. Try to arrange an R&R spot before you leave if you're on an extended jaunt, or wait to ask the locals when you arrive if you want to take your chances. Some places are more amenable to foreign housekeepers than others; a good local water supply helps (boil it if you're not sure), and local markets are one of the highlights of travel.

Don't forget to reconfirm

Always reconfirm flights. The usual time frame is seventy-two hours and most airlines accept calls before this; very few will accept calls after, and if the passenger list has been issued without your name on it, you stand a very good chance of missing the flight. If the flight is a weekly departure from Bombay to Nairobi on Saturdays only, and you have to connect with a prepaid safari on Monday, you could be in for a very expensive detour — or a lost safari.

When you phone to reconfirm, the airline asks for your address and phone number. Even if your current stop is for one night, that's the address you give. They are satisfied when they can fill in their blanks, and they really only need to know you're acknowledging your reservation (sometimes made months before). If flying Vancouver to London for a forty-eight hour stopover and then on to Athens, have your travel agent confirm both flights for you before you leave.

Another word of caution — get to the airport early! In these days of commonly overbooked flights, reconfirming doesn't assure you of a seat if you arrive just sixty minutes before takeoff of an international flight.

I wanted to present a bouquet of red roses to a clerk in the New Delhi American Express office when she accomplished the seemingly impossible. She managed to secure my seat on my Kenya Air flight from Bombay to Nairobi after I hadn't reconfirmed my flight in time and the New Delhi Kenya Air office had cancelled my reservation — and it was impossible to get through on the phone to Kenya Air's central office in Bombay. I don't know what the clerk did, but she told me to give her two hours, and when I nervously returned to the office, I was confirmed (in writing) on the incredibly crowded flight which was flying only once that week. I will be forever grateful to AMEX, New Delhi; I couldn't buy red roses because the office was closing, and because the clerk insisted I go to the Delhi airport early so I wouldn't jeopardize my connecting flight. Such is travel in India!

Chapter Nine

What to Take

Choosing a bag or backpack

Travel packs — the modern version of a backpack — are the ninety's boon to independent travelers. Unzip the cover that hides the straps, hoist the bag onto your back, and you can manage short connections over any terrain almost anywhere.

Bags on wheels with collapsible handles are the ultra modern way to go, but they have terrain limitations and their rigid frames can be cumbersome. The wheels work great over smooth corridors in airports, but not so well over uneven cobblestones or on rocky paths ascending to hillside pensions. And if you want the sides to collapse to squeeze into a tight train or plane compartment, you may have difficulties with the fixed perimeters.

Choose a travel pack that fits your needs as well as your body. Packs with internal frames need to be adjusted to your back after they are fully loaded. Estimate the weight you will be carrying, pack your bag, and have the store personnel bend the frame to fit. Buying from a knowledgeable sport or travel shop helps here. If purchasing a small pack with limited capacity, it may not be possible to adjust the internal frame, but you also will probably not have enough room if you need clothes for a variety of climates.

Smaller packs stay within carry-on limits (9 x 21 x 13 inches, 23 x 53 x 33cm), and often the best way to go is with two small packs — one day pack you can carry in front of you (loaded with your camera and other carry-on necessities), while your travel pack is on your back. Carry-on size is important if you are flying several interconnecting legs with little transfer time. If you are flying mostly direct nonstop destination flights, your bag will probably arrive with you if it is checked, and you can risk carrying a few more supplies in a more fully stuffed pack. Remember to have your camera and film readily accessible for hand inspection at airports, and for those last minute shots if loading onto a camel train.

Decide what size of pack you need and how durable it needs to be. Heavy coated Cordura nylon will stand a lot of rough handling and stay almost waterproof although zippers can draw water in a downpour. Cost is also a major consideration; luggage prices can soar out of sight, which most mature adventurers find an unnecessary expense. Durability, weight and comfort on your back are more important than expensive multi-pocketed matched pieces that rip easily and are difficult to carry. But don't underestimate your need to spend enough for a durable pack if you plan to do a lot of traveling. Buying cheaply will find you with a sore back plus rips and nicks in your bag; spending enough for a moderately priced pack will be one of the nicest things you can do for yourself.

Think about how you want to pack. Do you want several small compartments or just one separate space for shoes? One thing to watch for is a bag that packs nicely lying flat but bulges at the bottom when everything shifts as soon as the pack is vertical. Individual compartments and cinch straps help to distribute weight and keep you organized. Shop around and compare when you are ready to buy. The choice is yours, and there is a surprising array of styles and shapes from which to choose.

What to include, what to leave out

Choosing what to take for extended travel to several countries requires research about the cultures you are visiting — what is necessary attire for visiting churches or mosques? — and about the weather you can expect to experience — will you need long johns for a hike to ten thousand feet in the tropics? Deciding what to take on shorter trips seems less complicated, but the end results are surprisingly similar — one light-weight travel pack with the bare essentials for each place you are visiting.

Learning to travel light becomes an art. Reminisce about all those times you packed clothes (and gadgets) you didn't use on previous trips, and be ruthless with your new list. There is no doubt that self-laundry will be a necessity, so take clothes that dry quickly and that don't wrinkle. A mix and match of neutral colors in natural fabrics or blends greatly simplifies traveling. Two changes of casual clothes suffice; for the occasional dressy affair, roll up a crinkle skirt or permanent press pants and you will need little else unless you want formal dress for a gala opera performance at Milan. Even if you are traveling around the world with a carry-on, you can pack a silk shirt for your skirt or pants, plus a pair of dress sandals — men usually have a universal pair of leather shoes along — and you can attend theatre or opera anywhere. Of course, one can always buy a unique batik shirt or culottes along the way, and replacing T-shirts on the go becomes automatic. When I traveled around the world, I mailed souvenirs home whenever I was in secure mailing posts, the packing being discarded, faded, much-laundered T-shirts.

Sojourning in the tropics requires little more than swimsuits and shorts. A sarong that covers your knees is useful for visiting temples and churches where T-shirt tops are okay — no bare shoulders for women, and bare-chested men not allowed. Take along a nylon windbreaker for rain squalls, a cotton skirt or pants if you want, and leave everything else at home.

If you are stopping in Austria for spring skiing on your way to Passover week in Israel, clothes packed will be more diversified, but you can still keep it simple. For women, a pair of stretch pants and a ski sweater will get you through alpine evenings, and a silk tunic top over the same pants will take you to the opera in Tel Aviv. Roll up a cotton skirt, a silk shirt and some cotton pants; add a swimsuit for spas, your thermal underwear and two turtle necks, and you are away. If your ski suit is one piece, you may be able to wrap it around your skis in their ski bag. If it is two pieces, wear the jacket. You will need a cardigan or light fleece for cool evenings in Israel, so you may find that you have something that will perform double-duty in Austria as well. For men, the list is almost identical: a pair of wrinkle-proof casual pants for alpine and Middle East evening wear, a casual sweater top, cotton pants and shirts for Israel, swim trunks, long johns and two turtlenecks.

Underwear, socks, and sleepwear are all matters of personal preference. Pack polypropylene or silk sock liners if your plans include trekking and hiking boots. The quick-drying liners can be rinsed out at night and the heavier hiking socks can be worn for longer. And for most mature adventurers, a pair of high quality, soft, part-fabric (usually GoreTex or something similar), part-leather hiking shoes or boots are adequate for everything from wandering around local markets to eight-hour trekking days in Nepal. Those four-pound leather clunkers we insisted on wearing twenty years ago are no longer necessary unless you are planning long range wilderness backpacking while carrying a heavy load, which comes under a different heading from casual hiking.

Specific adventure travel such as wilderness backpacking requires specific equipment, and casual hiking boots or shoes are probably not sufficient. Before you decide on an adventure tour — kayaking, skiing, hiking, sailing, cycling — ask lots of questions about equipment requirements. If you are instructed to bring a sleeping bag, find out about weight; if you are going kayaking, find out what size waterproof stuff sacks you will need; if you are sailing in the tropics, ask if swim flippers are supplied so all you need to tote is your mask and snorkel. Often it's possible to rent equipment. I didn't want to carry my sleeping bag around

Which way? Adventuring by bike in Ireland

the world with me, so for my African camping safari I rented one in Nairobi (luckily I didn't wait until Arusha, Tanzania which has no such facilities) for a small fee. The bag was clean and warm, and I only had to transport it on two short bus rides.

Shoes pose a major concern for many travelers; sore feet can certainly spoil one's good time so make sure you have comfortable, broken-in walking shoes that are suitable for museums plus lots of walking over varied terrain. Soft-sided walking/hiking shoe/boots in a dark color that doesn't show dirt will go anywhere, do anything. Spray with waterproofing before you go. Take dress sandals for women, light weight casual leather shoes for men, and that's all you need. If you are visiting warm climates, add a pair of sport sandals — North Americans are recognized the world over by their Tevas. Wear socks for slippers, or pack lightweight leather or fabric slip-ons if you have room.

The key is: keep things simple. The more complicated your clothes are, the more complicated everything else becomes. If your favorite outfit has to have green shoes that can't be worn with anything else, leave it at home. It will be a welcome change when you return.

Gadgets for traveling come under two categories: necessary aides, and luxury nice-to-haves if you have room. Necessary items are: for the laundry, a flat rubber universal sink plug, an elastic clothesline, a ziplock bag of all-temperature washing soap (keep the bag to restock from small packages as you go); first-aid kit (see "The Healthy Traveler" chapter checklist, page 101), glasses, and medical supplies; face/wash cloth; small packets of Kleenex; toiletries (leave fancy perfumes and aftershaves at home) and handiwipes or babywipes; a collapsible cup; travel quartz alarm clock; Swiss army knife with cork screw and mini screwdriver; pocket high-power sport flashlight; inflatable neck pillow, eye shields, ear plugs; universal converter and/or plugs for electric razor; survival kit with candle, matches and/or butane lighter; travel umbrella. All of these items (except the umbrella) can be gathered together in a clear plastic travel "kit bag" (stuff Kleenex packets into empty sockets in your pack and keep necessary toiletries and medical supplies in your carry-on). If there is leftover space and unused weight allowance, add some nice-to-haves like a tube of spot remover, some extra flashlight batteries, hand-held mirror with a stand, synthetic towel, map "loop" or magnifying glass, pocket calculator/computer, immersion heater, binoculars.

Add your water purifier in its own pouch or bag, and pile all of these gadgets next to your pack in the weeks you are preparing for your trip. You will be surprised how everything fits together like a jigsaw puzzle. Survival items blend with everyday necessities for developing countries where luxurious frills are not only unnecessary but unusable. One always needs a book to read, but bedtime story hour may only happen by flashlight or with candles if the island generator shuts down at 9:00 P.M., and the sixty watt bulb you have so carefully packed has no juice.

Special effects: rainwear, personalized entertainment, photography

Visiting any country during its monsoon season means one thing for sure — you will get wet. Monsoon showers are usually sudden, warm, and drenching. Umbrellas help, but a rain poncho or raincoat works better. If you are in a warm climate, you and your pack plus your camera can stay cool and dry under a nylon or plastic poncho. Coated nylon is more durable than plastic, more expensive, and more flexible. It covers equipment better, and is worth the expense to keep your camera dry. Ponchos as well as plastic travel raincoats fold small and store in handy pouches. Ponchos are an all-in-one affair that let the air circulate around you; short raincoats call for rain pants as well as a hat for full protection, and then you will be very warm. A hint is to wear shorts which probably won't get wet, and sometimes open fabric sandals are better than shoes or boots.

Travel during the rainy seasons of many areas of the world (usually spring and fall) asks for little more than an umbrella. Mediterranean countries seem to specialize in folding travel umbrellas — Rhodes and Cyprus and Turkey all have rows and rows of shops selling umbrellas. Many countries have predictable shower times, either early morning, late afternoon, or during the night. If you want to stay out of the rain, plan your days around local weather. Perhaps afternoons are best for museums if you are near mountains that trap precipitation to produce afternoon showers. Avoid being exposed in thunder and lightning, no matter where you are. If you are caught in the open, make yourself as inconspicuous as possible (in a fetal position) under or near a low shelter — not next to a tree. As everyone knows, lightning strikes tall objects, and you are in danger if you are exposed and ungrounded.

While waiting out a rain shower, a personal entertainment center can entertain you. Cassettes and a mini radio/cassette player let you tune into local news and weather before you review your language tapes and after you have had your favorite Bach recital. Compared to CDs, cassettes are the easiest to carry

Market day in the rain, Sarlat, France

and the most readily available recording of local music. Carry a good quality set of earphones because they are difficult to replace or repair. Extra batteries are usually available, but take along at least a couple for emergency replacement. In some remote areas they are very expensive to purchase or may be unavailable, just when you really want some soothing music from home.

Books are about as necessary as socks; you can survive without them, but not very comfortably. Plan your library before you go so that you start with a couple of thick paper backs you have been waiting to read. The best way to continue a fresh reading supply as you go is to trade with fellow travelers. Many guesthouses and pensions around the world collect library contributions from their guests and offer a free exchange system. Sometimes there will be a nominal used-book charge, but it will be far cheaper

Basket entrepreneurs, Tonga

than retail prices in a store. Books are a very expensive commodity the world over. Don't pass up a bargain if you see one, and remember that you may travel for weeks before finding anything in English. Guidebooks are always part of a traveler's library, and they can be very heavy, so be aware of weight when choosing which to take along.

Photography equipment is a matter of personal choice and expertise as well as experience. A good quality 35mm single-lens reflex camera (SLR) with a zoom lens is probably the most versatile camera; if the SLR has autofocus and built-in flash, there is even greater versatility. Many travelers also carry a compact point-and-shoot for those quick candid shots. Camcorders are popular with some travelers, but many find them more a liability than an asset, and definitely a security problem. Many pockets are picked while hands and arms and eyes are diverted shooting videos.

Taking your own film supply is a must, not only because it is cheaper, but you know the film is in good condition. If you are away for several months, send your exposed film home to someone who will store it in their fridge or at least in a cool, dark place until you return.

Tripods are a matter of personal preference again. Often they are more of a nuisance than useful, and there is usually a way to improvise. There are many mini-tripods on the market; experiment before you take one with you.

Keep your camera equipment together in a compact carrying case along with extra film. One solution is to have a big enough fanny pack for your film supply. Carrying film in a lead-lined bag is not recommended by professionals; insist on hand inspection at airports. Most travel photographers rely on 200 ASA and 400 ASA film. The new system of dual-purpose film sold and processed by special laboratories (Seattle Film Works is one — see "Appendix E" for address) allows for both slides and prints to be made from the same film. This is an inexpensive way to take lots of pictures, then choose only your best slides for a show, and the very best negatives for print reproduction.

What to take checklist:

1) Choosing a bag or backpack

   Q. What is the backpack of the nineties?

   check: travel packs that fit your travel needs and your body, rolling suitcases and limitations

   Q. How do I choose a travel pack?

   check: custom fitting when loaded, carry-on versus checked bag size, durability and portability, price

2) What to pack

   Q. What clothes should I take?

   check: cultural dress requirements, weather requirements, adventure tour needs

Q. How can I pack light?

check: laundry requirements, coordinated colors, natural or blended fabrics, two basic changes of clothes plus skirt or pants for dress, swimsuit, personal preferences of underwear and socks and sleepwear, hiking sock liners

Q. What shoes should I take?

check: fabric/leather combination in light weight hiking shoe or boot, dress sandals for women and casual leather shoes for men, sport sandals for hot climates

Q. What about specific equipment for adventure travel?

check: tour company's list very carefully, rental availability

Q. What gadgets are necessities?

check: kit bag for laundry supplies and universal plug, survival candle and matches, collapsible cup, Swiss army knife, electrical adaptors for razor

check: flashlight, water purifier, wash cloth, Kleenex, handiwipes, inflatable pillow, eye shields, ear plugs, clock, umbrella

Q. What additional supplies are nice to have?

check: spot remover, batteries, mirror, towel, immersion heater, magnifying glass, pocket computer/calculator, binoculars

3) Special effects

Q. What is the best equipment for monsoon climates?

check: ponchos versus rain coats, coated nylon versus plastic, open sandals versus shoes, shorts versus long pants

Q. What about showers?

check: umbrella, shower times, rainy day activities, electrical storm precautions

Q. What do I need for personal entertainment?

check: mini cassette/radio with earphones, language tapes, extra batteries

check: book supply, guidebooks, travel games

Q. What about travel photography?

check: 35mm single-lens reflex camera with zoom lens, autofocus, and flash

check: point-and-shoot compact, flash requirements, tripod, camcorder

check: film supply and speed, storage, carrying case, dual-purpose film

check: one camera bag for all equipment, film storage bag

Chapter Ten

Itineraries

Two weeks on foot in the Austrian Alps

Day hikes from a centrally located gasthof-pension for one week. For spectacular scenery, relatively easy hiking and a variety of terrain choose from: the Vorarlberg area, the Innsbruck-Igles or Mayrhofen regions of the Tyrol or the mountains of Kärnten near Klagenfurt.

Day 1:

Fly to Munich; pick up prearranged rental car; drive autobahn to Austria (approximately two hours) to prearranged gasthof-pension reserved through the Austrian National Tourist Office, 500 Fifth Avenue, New York, NY 10110 or 11601 Wilshire Boulevard, Suite 2480, Los Angeles, CA 90025 or 2 Bloor Street East, Suite 3330, Toronto, Ontario M4W 1A8 or Suite 1220-1223, Vancouver Block, Vancouver, BC V6Z 1J2 *or* take public bus to destination city.

This will be a long day but the drive is not difficult, and Munich is the closest major gateway to the mountains. Over-

Checking maps in the Vorarlberg, Austria

night near the Munich airport if you won't have enough daylight to find your gasthof-pension. Zurich is an alternative and close to the Vorarlberg province; Vienna is a possibility if you want to visit Vienna first, pick up a car and head for the Klagenfurt region for hiking, up to Innsbruck for hiking, over to Salzburg and the Salzkammergut for sightseeing and more hiking, then back to Vienna (this will take more than two weeks).

If you are flying from North America directly to Munich, you will need more than one day of acclimatizing before you begin hiking — give yourself enough extra time.

Day 2:

Rest. Relax in gasthof. Wander about town. Get hiking trail maps from local tourist information office. Initiate yourself with a schnitzel and beer dinner.

Day 3:

Day hike. Keep it short. Enjoy a lunch break at an alms house.

Day 4:

Day hike. End the day in a spa/pool — there is bound to be one nearby.

Day 5:

Day hike. Gain more elevation, perhaps up to a hütte for a goulash lunch.

Day 6:

Day hike — or rest — or shopping — or all three.

Day 7:

Drive or bus to next area. Arrange gasthof-pension through local tourist information desk (unless you are in high season of July, August, and early September when you may want to book ahead).

Days 8, 9, 10, 11:

Same as days 3, 4, 5, 6.

Day 12:

Long day hike. Get up to a hütte for sure.

Day 13:

Drive to Munich and overnight near airport if you have an early departure time. Farewell schnitzel dinner.

Day 14:

Fly home.

Five weeks by car in Italy

Driving is possible in Italy if you are a little brave, and if you stay out of cities. Italy is a land of churches, art, and history and it is nice to have the freedom of a car to accommodate museums' mid-day closures, unexpected special exhibits, or even an appearance of the Pope. You can stop at a friendly vineyard whenever you please, or sit by the sea soaking up the atmosphere. Learn all about Michelangelo in Florence and Rome; Venetian glass blowing and serenading gondoliers are not to be missed in Venice. This itinerary can begin and end anywhere in Italy, but I have chosen Venice because it is well serviced by public transportation (direct flights from London) and also negotiable by car which you will probably pick up at the airport. Look into leasing if taking a car for more than three weeks. Make sure you have a good map or two, and that you understand Italian road signs — autostrada direction signs are green, secondary road signs are blue. It is possible to drive Italy's autostrada from Lichtenstein to the tip of the boot, but the tolls are high, speed is fast (not as fast as Germany's autobahn), and air pollution is often a thick brown pall hanging over the highway. Use secondary roads when you can; watch for tractors and sheep and bicycles. From gondolas to lemon groves to the Sistine Chapel to Chianti Classico — *Ciao*!

Days 1 to 6:

Venice.

Day 7:

Pick up car, drive to Tuscany to pre-booked farm or villa or apartment.

Days 8 to 14:

Explore Tuscany — Florence via bus from Greve, Pisa, Sienna, wineries, don't miss hill town of Monteriggioni.

Day 15:

Drive to Perugia.

Days 15, 16, 17:

Explore Perugia, Gubbio, Assisi.

Day 18:

Drive to outskirts of Rome — Castel Gandolfo is easily reached by car, and train into Rome.

Days 19 to 22:

Rome.

Day 23:

Drive to Amalfi Coast (pick up a large-scale local map).

Days 24 to 28:

Explore Ravello, Almalfi, Positano, Massa Lubrense, Marina di Puolo.

Day 29:

Sorrento and Capri.

Day 30:

Drive the Appenines via Pompei.

Days 30 to 32:

Explore Abruzzo National Park, lace making at Pescostanzo, L'Aquila, Gran Sasso.

Day 33:

Drive to Arezzo, ask tourist office for local maps and directions to Michelangelo's birthplace "Caprese Michelangelo" (45 km NE), and ask locals for birthplace/museum access.

There is a road somewhere, Amalfi coast, Italy

Day 34:

Drive to Treviso.

Day 35:

Return car. Say farewell to Italy until the next time—it is addicting!

Ten months around the world

The size of the world depends on one's perspective. Since it is possible to fly around the globe in less than ten days, taking ten months can be tediously long for some, incredibly short for others. For inveterate travelers, even ten long months will go too quickly, with many sites remaining on their "must come back for" list. The following itinerary is merely a suggestion for planning continuous travel in a westward direction, including major destination tours and rest stops on the way. The trip covers ten months because of weather considerations; sites include some wonders of the world, along with a few surprises. If you want to travel all the way around, list those places you have always wanted to see and connect them with a string across a map of the world. Study weather patterns, find a helpful flight consolidator, and soon you will be vagabonding. See chapter on "Planning" (page 35) for more hints.

Planning a trip of this magnitude takes time — at least six months, preferably a year. Whatever you do, don't rush. Tackle as many countries as you think you will enjoy, then start making lists. Financial planning will be the most essential phase because travel anywhere in today's world costs a lot — always more than we think, although Turkey is still affordable, so don't wait to put it on your itinerary, whenever you go.

September 1:

Fly from west coast of North America to South Pacific: Tahiti for 10 days, includes the tropical wonders of Bora Bora and Moorea; Fiji for 10 days, includes inter-island pass to the garden isle of Teveuni plus two other islands; Tonga for 8 days, includes Tonga Tapu and the Vava'u islands for sailing, snorkeling, and an *umu* (local feast). Don't plan anything for a Sunday in Tonga because it's a religious day of rest for everyone, including airline pilots.

October:

New Zealand. Fly to Christchurch on the South Island, rent a car, tour island, hike on the glaciers, visit penguins; cross Cook Strait, tour the North Island including the Bay of Islands and Cape Reinga and the kauri forest and museum, climb some pas, enjoy Auckland's museums, return car and fly Auckland to Australia. Take time for a few days rest and respite on a beach.

November:

One month in Australia — it's up to you, but don't miss at least some of the outstanding wineries. Take in a sheep auction as well as a shearing, along with the Wool Museum at Geelong. Treat yourself to a performance at the Sydney Opera House, and of course, the beach culture has to be experienced to appreciate it. The Great Barrier Reef and Ayers Rock are Aussieland's two

Australia's showpiece, Sydney Opera House and harbour

main attractions, but there's lots more if you want to skip them. You need a visa for entry into Australia.

December:

Indonesia in monsoon season. Take your poncho. Arrange a tour to Camp Leakey, Kalimantan if you want to see the orang-utans. Book an air pass before leaving home. Spend at least a week on Bali (don't miss a cremation), a few days in Yogyakarta (avoid Jakarta at all costs; try to fly in and out of Denpasar); try to get to Sulawesi and Irian Jaya.

December 31

New Year's Eve in Singapore! Don't stay long because it's too expensive.

January first two weeks:

Malaysia. Historic Melakka, the cool Cameron Highlands, Pangkor Island on the west coast or Tioman on the east coast, Penang for gateway to Thailand and Thai visa and bus.

January second two weeks plus first week of February:

Thailand. Rest and respite at Kho Phi Phi; ferry to Phuket. Fly north, visit hill tribes, Chiang Rai and Chiang Mai, return to Bangkok where three days is enough. Fly to Kathmandu and obtain visa upon arrival.

Mid February:

Nepal. Buy some wool scarves for warmth. Trek Kathmandu valley, river raft to Chitwan National Park hoping to see a tiger, several days at Pokhara, fly to Delhi. Visas required for India.

End of February, beginning of March:

India. Tour Delhi and Golden Triangle via hired car and driver. The land of contrasts and the Taj Mahal at last! Obtain necessary visas for East Africa in Delhi. Fly Delhi to Nairobi, Kenya.

March:

East Africa. Tanzania wildlife safari; camping with the lions. Photos and more photos. Thrilling sights of nature's wonders of the world in their natural habitats.

April:

The Middle East. Egypt for two weeks of pyramids and temples and cruising on the Nile, more wonders of the world. Israel and Jordan tour from historical Jerusalem to ancient monasteries at Petra. Overnight ferry Haifa to Limassol, Cyprus.

First two weeks of April:

Rest and respite on beautiful Cyprus. Oranges and Aphrodite, mosaics and Greek Orthodox monasteries. Rent a car for a few days. Overnight ferry to Rhodes, Greece.

Middle week of April:

A beautiful island in the Aegean for sun, biking, the magic of Athena's Temple at Lindos. Hydrofoil (45 minutes) Rhodos to Marmaris, Turkey.

Aphrodisias, still the city of love, Turkey

Remaining weeks of April and May:

Turkey. Rent a car or take the dolmus. Visit Pamukkale, Konya, Cappadocia, Ankara for the Museum of Anatolia, Istanbul, Ephesus and Selçuk. Rest and respite at a fishing village on the coast. Splurge for a grand finale and cruise the Lycian coast aboard a gulette. Return to Rhodes for flight to Athens and North America.

Appendix A

Travel Literature

Newsletters

Cast Travel News by Canadian Association of Senior Travelers, 1543 Bayview Avenue, Suite 301, Toronto, ON, M4G 3B5, Canada

Connecting for single travelers, PO Box 29088, 1996 West Broadway, Vancouver, BC, V6J 5C2, Canada

Freighter Travel News, 3524 Harts Lake Road, Roy, WA 98580, USA

International Living, Agora Inc., 105 West Monument Street, Baltimore, MD 21201, USA (American and Canadian editions)

Travel Scoop: the Independent Traveler's Newsletter, 1110 Yonge Street, Suite 200, Toronto, ON, M4W 2L6, Canada

TravLtips Cruise and Freighter Travel Association, 163-07 Depot Road, PO Box 580218, Flushing, New York 11358, USA

Rick Steves' *Europe Through the Back Door Newscat*, 120 Fourth Avenue North, PO Box 2009, Edmonds, WA 98020-2009 USA. Phone (206) 771-8303 for free copy.

Books

A Journey of One's Own: Uncommon advice for the Independent Woman Traveler, Thalia Zepatos, The Eighth Mountain Press, Portland, Oregon, 1992.

Do's and Taboos of Preparing for Your Trip Abroad, Roger E. Axtell and John P. Healy, John Wiley & Sons, Inc., 1994

Free to Travel, The Canadian Guide for 50 Plus Travelers, Pam Hobbs & Michael Algar, Doubleday Canada, 1994.

International Travel Weather Guide, Tom Hoffman and Randy Mann, Weather Press, PO Box 660606, Sacramento, CA 95866, USA

Pamphlets

Bon Voyage, But ... Tips for Canadians Traveling Abroad, Info Center, Department of Foreign Affairs and International Trade, 125 Sussex Drive, Ottawa, ON, Canada, K1A 0G2, phone (800) 267-6788

Key Officers of Foreign Service Posts by the US State Department, US Government Printing Office, PO Box 371954, Pittsburgh, PA 15250, phone (202) 783-4818

Appendix B

Medical Travel Resources

CDC (US Centers for Disease Control) hotline (404) 332-4559 (from US and Canada)

CDC FAX Information Service, (404) 332-4565 (follow prompts to receive documents)

Don't Drink the Water, the complete traveler's guide to staying healthy in warm climates, co-published by Canada Public Health Association and Canadian Society for International Health, 400-1565 Carling Avenue, Ottawa, ON, K1Z 8R1, phone (613) 725-3769

Health Information for International Travel, US Department of Health and Human Services, Public Health Service, Superintendent of Documents, US Government Printing Office, Washington, DC 20402, phone (202) 783-3238. Also available from Renouf Publishing Co., 1294 Algoma Road, Ottawa, ON, K1B 3W8, Canada

IAMAT, International Association for Medical Assistance to Travelers, 40 Regal Road, Guelph, ON, N1K 1B5, Canada, phone (519) 836-0102, and 417 Center Street, Lewiston, New York 14092, USA, phone (716) 754-4883

STERI-AID sterile medical travel kit, PO Box 81614, 1057 Steeles Avenue West, North York, ON, M2R 3X1, Canada

The Pocket Doctor, Stephen Bezruchka, MD, The Mountaineers, 1011 SW Klickitat Way, Suite 107, Seattle, WA 98134, USA. Also available from Douglas & McIntyre, Ltd., 1615 Venables Street, Vancouver, BC, V5L 2H1, Canada

Appendix C

House Exchange Organizations

Canadian Teacher's Home Exchange, 264 Fairmont Avenue, Ottawa, ON, K14 1Y2, phone (613) 722-3252

Intervac Canada, 606 Alexander Crescent NW, Calgary, AB, T2M 4T3, phone (403) 284-3747

Trading Homes, 413-1189 Westwood Street, Coquitlam, BC, V3B 4S6, phone (604) 464-7984

Landfair Home Exchange Club, 54 Landfair Crescent, Scarboro, ON, M1J 3A7, phone (416) 431-4493

Worldhomes Holiday Exchange, 1707 Platt Crescent, North Vancouver, BC, V7J 1X9, phone (604) 987-3262

Trade to Travel, 20100 Courthouse Road, Yale, VA, 23897 USA

Vacation Exchange Club, PO Box 650, Key West, Florida, USA, phone (800) 638-3841

Vacation Homes Unlimited, 18547 Soledad, Suite 223, Santa Clarita, CA 91351, phone (805) 848 7927

Appendix D

Adventure Groups

Ecosummer Expeditions, 1516 Duranleau Street, Vancouver, BC, V6H 3S4, Canada, phone (800) 465-8884, fax (604) 669-3244

Elderhostel Canada, 308 Wellington Street, Kingston, ON, K7K 7A7

Elderhostel USA, 75 Federal Street, Boston, MA, 02110

ElderTreks, 597 Markham Street, Toronto, ON, M6G 2L7, phone (800) 741-7956

Explore Trek Holidays, 8412 – 109 Street, Edmonton, AB, T6G 1E2, Canada, phone (403) 439-9118, fax (403) 433-5494

Interhostel, University of New Hampshire, 6 Garrison Avenue, Durham, NH, 03824-3529, USA

Appendix E

Travel Resources

American Society of Travel Agents (ASTA), World Headquarters Department of Consumer Affairs, Alexandria, VA, phone (703) 706-0386

International Air Travel Association, 2000 Peel Street, Montreal, PQ, H3A 2R4, Canada

National Tour Association (NTA), PO Box 3071, Lexington, KY 40596-3071, USA

Eurobus, represented in US and Canada by Eurotrips, Inc., 8 South J Street, PO Box 1288, Lake Worth, FL 33460-1288, USA, phone (407) 582-7982, fax (407) 582-1581

Seattle Film Works, Elliot Bay at Pier 89, 1260 – 16th Avenue West, Seattle, WA 98119, USA

Canadian Department of Foreign Affairs hotline for current conditions in specific countries (800) 267-6788

US State Department hotline (202) 647-5225